THE
SANCTITY
& PROFANITY OF
SEXUALITY

AN EXPLORATION OF ALL
ASPECTS OF EROTICISM

ANTHONY WAKEFIELD HILL

THE
SANCTITY
& PROFANITY OF
SEXUALITY

AN EXPLORATION OF ALL
ASPECTS OF EROTICISM

MEMOIRS
Cirencester

PUBLISHED TITLES

Parsifal's Journal, Issue 1
Being the Life and Concerns of Christ

The One and the Many
A Book of Aphorisms

The Knowledge of Everything
According to the Voice of the Silence

Journey to the Centre of the Cosmos
A brief summary of the work, to date,
of Anthony Wakefield Hill

The Sanctity and Profanity of Sexuality
An Exploration of all Aspects of Eroticism

(See the rear of the book for forthcoming titles.)

MEMOIRS
PUBLISHING

Published by Memoirs

1A The Wool Market Cirencester Gloucestershire GL7 2PR
info@memoirsbooks.co.uk   www.memoirspublishing.com

The Sanctity and Profanity of Sexuality
An Exploration of All Aspects of Eroticism

ISBN: 978-1-909874-41-1

"PLEASURE IS LOVE
AND LOVE PLEASURE,
AND LOVE THE ONLY THING THAT
ENOBLES IT."

Fanny Hill

CONTENTS

FOREWORD

I beg the reader to read both the Preface, and the book as a whole, right through from the first word to the last, because unless he does so, he will not have a clue what the book is about. All my works depend on a logical argument running from start to finish, meaning that if one step is left out, the argument falls apart and the message is not understood. It would be most unintelligent to 'scan' my books, or jump from place to place, leaving out pages or even paragraphs and sentences; the work must be treated as an integral whole, as my method is 'progressive amplification', or 'cumulative illustration'. These terms are self-explanatory; 'progressive' means 'by stages', 'cumulative' means 'adding up to'; put the two together and you have an amplification, or illustration, that by stages adds up to proof.

One of the main concerns in the present volume being that of Good and Evil, it will perhaps be confusing to find that the author appears to contradict himself in certain passages; this is because some passages were written before others while being included at a later date; thus the meaning of Evil as opposed to wickedness is sometimes obscured. The reader should therefore, if in doubt, remember that the meaning of Evil, as outlined in the Preface, page iii, has been acquired comparatively recently by the author, and in some excerpts retains its conventional and traditional concept. The author apologizes for this shortcoming.

PREFACE

We make love by love, with love, in love, and for love.

Let me start out by saying that this is a book about love—not sex (whatever that might mean). In the first issue of 'Parsifal's Journal', I titled the relevant essay 'sex': by 'sex' I meant love, but in deference to what most people mean by love, I decided to use the lesser term.

The opening statement was as follows: "The idea that sex is for pleasure is a total, and disastrous, illusion." How anyone can interpret that as a recipe for pornography defies the imagination; but that is precisely what has happened. This most honourable of essays has been condemned as licentious, immoral, and beyond the pale—in fact the police have threatened to charge me with 'obscenity'. It just goes to show what an unintelligent lot you readers are; one myopic look at a 'rude word,' and you shriek for the nearest policeman.

In fact, I use 'rude words' for a very specific reason; far from being a pornographer, it was my express intention, in that essay, to revive the innocence of sex—by re-introducing love to a jaded world. (I did, incidentally, lose my girl-friend because of her inability to see this.) It was my further intention to re-introduce Anglo-Saxon words to the same end, coupling them with explicit sexual references in order to re-design the whole of civilisation in relation to its erotic culture.

Running through the whole of this present book, in particular connection with sexuality, is the notion of Good and Evil, the paramount pair of opposites, the study of which has the power to produce the knowledge of everything. In the desire to restore man's innocence, I am drawing together goodness and evil from the opposite ends of the earth—a most almighty task; respect me for it.

Every schoolgirl and every schoolboy, from here to Timbuktu, will thank me; every hard-pressed wife, and every harassed husband, will die in gratitude; and, one day, I might be acknowledged by the Church itself. Let, therefore, the Law and Mary Whitehouse stand back.

I am educating the world in innocent sexuality, and my purpose in using explicit terms and descriptions is to bring the reader to consciousness; by using explicit words I am making explicit that which they represent; in other words, I am making it real for the first time. Do not dismiss as pornography what is actually the initial Anglo-Saxon—the original reality—which I so dearly desire to give you. In shocking you I hope to introduce you to life. In addition, by becoming real yourself *you will begin to exist;* explicitness produces thought, thought produces existence; in the words of the sage, "I think, therefore I am". I am of course referring to the process of individuation, which is the state of individuality, or psychological reality, brought about by consciousness; in becoming real, one sees and, in seeing, one exists, or lives for the first time. In making these things explicit I am raising your consciousness and rendering you aware of them; *in being aware, you think, or see.*

The twin parameters of Loving and Learning are in fact inseparable in any exposition of either, love and consciousness receiving unavoidably equal attention throughout my work.

In the statement "The idea that sex is for pleasure is a total, and disastrous, illusion," I mean to convey that, though the means of sex is pleasure, the purpose of sex is love; and in the failure to realise this vital and fundamental truth lies the whole disaster of our sexual history. People go into sex thinking, "I'm going to have a bloody good time," but unless you approach sex from the point of view of its purpose, rather than the means, you will destroy yourself, your lover and sex itself. Sex must be sacrificed initially, to be found again *within* love: its end *and* beginning.

My personal investigation has led me to the door of 'The Flowers of Evil,' a subject first addressed, of course, by Baudelaire, though indirectly, incompletely and without a true knowledge of its significance. Poets sense things without necessarily being conscious of them. Both Baudelaire and I celebrate evil—for the very best of reasons. *Once again I stress the difference between 'evil', which is almost virtuous or innocent, and 'wickedness.' Man will find his release in the acceptance of evil—in its purity, its beauty, and its rightness and quintessential employment in love, where it finds its ultimate resolution and transfiguration. But even in everyday life, the naturalness of evil finds acceptance if one regards good and evil merely as manifestations of positivity and negativity—two atomic polarities as found in every physical and mental phenomenon. Wickedness remains wickedness, and that is what Christ has come to expunge.*

Thus, the whole historical problem of Good and Evil is solved. No longer will man be under the illusion that God punishes evil. Nor does he punish wickedness, for he has sent his Son into the world to take the rap for man's sins. By appearing to be punished for the sins of mankind, Christ is taking upon himself the suffering and wickedness of man, in order to demonstrate not God's anger, but His great love.

Raise roses from the bed of manure—flowers sprung from evil.

*   *   *

Now a short example in which we pursue the whole gamut of love and lust intertwined, finally merging into the mysterious One Moment. The employment of explicit words is essential to my purpose (as already expressed) particularly as contrasted with the finer sentiments.

I FUCK WITH MY HEART

Let us be rude together; let us fuck our way into the dark daylight of paradise.

The colours of sportiveness will manifest themselves as light and dark, cool and warm; knickers will fly off, kisses will abound, with drooling lips and dripping thighs. Much stroking of parts will there be as excitement rises on the tide of ecstasy; my sweetheart swoons as, meeting me frantically, she succumbs to the delirium of fevered delight.

Ah, God, what heaven it is to be alive, Divesting her of her hot and intimate panties for the second time, I copiously kiss her lovely young breasts, increasing the flow of lava from her vulva; and, whispering the most endearing sweet nothings in her gentle ears, I charm that sensitive soul to even greater ecstasy than the skill of my hand is able. Lust and love become fused in Desire, love piling on lust, lust piling on love, until, eventually, they are indistinguishable—a true Union after the initial segregation, Mother and Whore being reconciled as One.

Her eyes misty, her cheeks rosy with ardour, she closes the Parts with me: man to woman, lover to mistress, genitals upon genitals, spirit upon flesh—all and everything meets in Love—love the final arbiter and integrator, after love's—yes, love's,—disintegration. For, in order to integrate, we have first to disintegrate—

disintegrate in order to see. And thus, it is heaven to be alive.

To those who would condemn me, I would say that, always and everywhere, I stress the predominance and sacredness of love; let that never be forgotten.

*   *   *

What is God's to give is God's to take away.

And so God doth extract Carnality from the universe, along with Physics—the science of the urbane—and every example of venereal wit set up to glorify the illusion of Humankind.

In, by, for and through love, do we make love: Love, the only reality.

Through the study of love—in other words, the reality of good and evil—do we discover Child, Father, Mother and Whore.

One in All, All in One.

(Message from Tenerife)

Lo, tis love that governs us—that governs all. From that initial, o' so chaste kiss to denuding her of her nether garments, l' amour c'est que j'aime. For, nothing else exists, except that Spirit, divinely given from on high, divinely implemented, within which all pleasure, all carnal grossness, disappears—that spirit which both rises to the heights and descends to the depths, on the one hand dragging flesh up to heaven, on the other dragging spirit down to carnality. That which hovers above, and between, distils the vapours of purity, redeeming both spirit and flesh and meeting them, each to each, half-way.

Love it is that makes it possible for the One to be converted into the one, or the Collective into the individual; similarly, the One Spirit, or Collective Spirit, becomes converted into the one spirit, or individual spirit. The common denominator is consciousness——or the conscious-unconscious divide——creating the vertical edifice of individual evolution as opposed to the horizontal plateau of collectivity; the conscious-unconscious divide is the River Rubicon, which, once it has been crossed from unconsciousness into consciousness, cannot be re-crossed; the transition into consciousness, or individuality, is irrevocable. The transforming power, from the collective to the individual, is Love, in all the vast knowledge and ability at its command.

It is because of the irrevocability of the transition into consciousness, facilitated by love, that modern man cannot, without destroying civilisation itself, regress to the state of unity, or collectivity—civilisation being the state of individuality. *Paradise has been lost. But Paradise can be regained.* The first law of civilisation is "to free ourselves from identification with the One;" the first law is, at the same time, "to become united with that One." Of course, the two are mutually exclusive; *but they must be realised. They can be realised through the truly irrational, or mystical, Union of Opposites.*

The original state of Unity, in which everything was whole and magical—the condition of 'Participation Mystique'—first disintegrates into anarchy and violence of all kinds, then, through an amalgam of consciousness, Love and the Irrational, it gives way to the final goal of Union, or the re-integrated state of civilisation.

It is love that leads us, love that guides us, love that nurtures us—all the way, from the first moments to the last; unless sex is approached from the point of view of love, it is doomed to destruction.

It is the Spiritual-Body that makes us, and keeps us, whole; only the purest love will mend the carnal body. Existence is a place we visit—the body, a place we are guests within; let us show it respect. Indeed it is an illusion, but an honourable illusion, deserving of the ways of love to give it meaning and wholeness.

By virtue of love, the body is whole; hers is given in trust to you: she doesn't want to be undignified, she doesn't want to be ugly; and in love, the body is united to heart, soul and mind, through which its wholeness is established. Element is united to element, part is united to whole; each fragment—each tissue—is given its individual dignity; and all the while we remember that the whole is far more than the sum of its parts—giving itself with infinite gracefulness.

The sight of the body's appurtenances is designed to excite; yet it is not what we see that moves us: we are moved by the *meaning* of what we see; the greater part of what we see lies behind the object, in the hinterland of Mind. The body is a symbol, containing many symbols. And behind Mind lies Love. Love it is that signals, Love that determines what we do, how our bodies disport. And Love is infinitely personal, knowing no divergence from selfhood—self to self, person to person—aware only of respect for the other. It is Love that tells her to open her legs, to invite you in—not an 'idea', an extraneous fantasy. Love dictates how playmates engage.

In illicit sex, those buttocks, those breasts, would not be hers; they would be anybody's—a prey to lust. No personal meaning here—just flesh amid the flesh-pots; the body cries in despair as it is subjected to yet another night of infamy, another anonymous assault, which comes not from the Mind, but from the void. If you want your breasts, your buttocks, to be viewed as insensible objects, just surrender yourself to your boyfriend's straying hands, and acquiesce to his lewd immaturity. Many a hitherto lovely and virtuous girl has done this, and been turned, quite against her nature, into a vicious whore. Of how many is that so devastatingly true?

The Spiritual-Body and the carnal body have a

unique relationship; the spiritual-body lifts the carnal right out of physical gravity, yet the carnal body retains its gravitas (as opposed to gravity). But the Divine, or spiritual, Body, being a combination of the physical and spiritual, floats above carnality, being of it yet not within it. *Be aware of paradox.*

The Divine Body is the handmaiden of Love, implementing it, substantiating it—at the same time, etherealising it—and keeping Love's functions pure: the river of Libido, of which the Divine-Body is a guise, runs clear, suffusing all things with its essence, and freeing the physical world of turgid muddiness.

With constant practice, it is possible to achieve aloofness from physicality, within the Spiritual-Body; one continues within the physical world, but one is not immured in it.

I do not desire pleasure: I desire the pleasure of my sweetheart's company. Those buttocks are not anybody's, those breasts are not anybody's; they are unique between *us*; and love makes them temperate.

Her buttocks and breasts belong to the one, individual, body as opposed to the One, Collective, Body. Love makes it possible to linger within the carnal body without activating its grosser levels; individuality confers independence of the ties to the physical, and collective, body where carnality is compulsive.

TRIBUTE TO TERESA

It is the impersonal that God can't stand; she can dance all night—as long as she likes—but she is so lovely in her innocence—her Person—that she could do no wrong; and in my arms, afterwards, we would celebrate what God put us on earth for: *to enjoy each other's love*—pleasure subordinated tenfold.

Those buttocks, half revealed by scanty panties, are meant for me alone—ravishing in their voluptuous beauty, and all the more beautiful for being mine. Moved to white hot heat, we couple in the ecstasy of Love's Personality.

Buttocks are indeed to be enjoyed—especially Teresa's, along with the rest of her divine body—symbolic, as they are, of the *inner* charms of love.

*   *   *

As we said above, it is possible to achieve aloofness from the physical world, through the Spiritual-Body; that is to say, through contemplation of the Spiritual-Body, or *the cathartic-image*. For the Divine, or Spiritual, Body sublimates, or transubstantiates, the grossly physical aspects of existence; in fact it lifts the body right out of existence into the Divine Life. Through contemplation of the cathartic image, and of the philosophy surrounding it, one learns the true facts of life and that man, if he is diligent, can inherit the earth. *For the Divine Life and the earthly life are one*—if the earthly life is sublimated. Earthly life may continue unmolested when its venereal, or fleshly, attributes are expunged and it experiences transfiguration.

THE PUBIC REGION

That less than beautiful area sets off the rest of her loveliness, and, by association, receives beauty in return, knowing nothing less in the eyes of the girl's lover.

Her eyes speak of love, desire subordinated, whole waking whole, or the whole of the mind waking the whole of the body—pubic region included, which receives the beauty of the rest of the body through the body's totality.

LOVE AND THE DISTRIBUTION OF ENERGY

The Whore is energy personified; the runaway whore— the illicit whore—is raw energy in an uncontrolled state. In sex, love is what controls energy; from two points of view. First, in sexual intercourse, second, in the philosophy derived from the restraint of love.

Civilisation is based on the constraint, or conservation, of energy, served quintessentially by love;

it is every man's duty as a citizen to conserve the collective body of energy through attention to his personal love-life; let not the Whore run away with you. Furthermore it is also every man's duty to subject his love-life to the most minute examination, over a prolonged period—if necessary, to renounce sex for, again, an extended period; if one wants to learn all, one must sacrifice all.

In the conservation of energy—in other words, libido—is involved the process of individuation, including both will and consciousness; to sacrifice love—or sex—requires will, and through the exercise of will one also achieves consciousness: "To Love and to Learn" is the watchword of culture; it might read, "To *will* and to learn." By subjecting one's energy to brutal suppression, one erects the structure of individuality, or the accumulation of consciousness; the associated method is by 'psychological differentiation', which comes about as a result of general consciousness, that including the separating of psychological functions, thus collating the whole of the psyche in its explicated totality. By my method of direct assault on one's natural energy, one wins one's spurs in the Battle for Life. (By 'self-suppression,' of course, I do not mean '*self-repression*', which is pathological.)

* * *

Buttocks become dissociated when energy becomes concentrated in them, instead of being distributed around the body; flesh becomes moribund, and buttocks resemble nothing so much as pork from the butcher's shambles; Libido is thus dammed up in a murky morass.

The round voluptuousness of the nether regions, so delightful to the eye of the amorous beholder, and only half concealed by her scanties, is something to die for, *as part of her. The 'quickened flesh' is what we seek—the living whole of body within mind.*

What the buttocks lead to is the soul, or mind, the soul being the activator of the mind, and also of the body; my girl's bottom, charming though it is, is but a stepping-stone to the meeting of two souls, a place which we visit for a hot dalliance prior to the main business of love. The bottom may be a focal area of the body—just as every other area of the body—but, in fact, the body is provided as the vehicle for love, not as the main focus of love, *which speaks to us through the eyes, the window of the soul.*

When I invite her to play with me, I am not asking her just to 'play with my cock;' I am asking her to play with *me, also—my self, in its wholeness*

THE HINTERLAND OF LOVE

Love lives on the *inside*—the inside of the body and the mind, where true emotion takes place; the body is the exterior, and obvious, place of love.

Teresa dances only for me, in the midnight interior, armed with panties, bra and o' so short skirt showing a hint of the naughty parts. How I love her; "Play with me, my darling; let me feast my eyes on your glorious body."

In the interior resides the Divine Form, hidden yet glowing, making itself visible through the body and bodily activities, but, internally, giving meaning in the night-time embers; look inward and you will find the 'Philosopher's Gold', shining in the dark, where Teresa's divine little form is gently suggested, and her presence felt most strongly.

The exterior of the mind coincides with the body, *while remaining distinct*; Teresa dances both internally and externally, *yet only internally*—for my pleasure, with her love. Only the mind is real, for it is exclusively internal and yet contains both inner and outer; solely by accepting this quadruple relationship can one understand the paradox of the Psyche.

So Teresa dances on in the innocence born of the internal reality of Love.

*   *   *

Nothing but the Spiritual-Body can heal the divide between essence and existence, or spirit and body; that is, there is no reality but the Spiritual-Body; there is no other means of furthering evolution. Spirit has no existence, nor has body, except as belonging to each other, and then only by virtue of the Third Element—rising between, but not being of, both (the Spiritual-Body and the Third Element are, in this respect, synonymous).

If spirit and body existed by the mere fact of belonging to each other, the modern, civilised, world itself would not exist; for, when the opposites know no difference between themselves, *there is no existence at all. Existence occurs only when that which exists sees a reflection of itself; in other words, "I see myself, therefore I am"*.

The Third Element, or Spiritual-Body, has to arise between the two opposites, first to separate them, then to re-unite them, thus nailing them to the Cross of existence, initially and, finally, bringing them to the promise of Eternal Life.

*   *   *

In this Preface I have tried to point up two things: the antimony of spirit and flesh, or sacred and profane love, *neither being omitted from the other*; we have spiritual, though fleshly, love, and fleshly, though spiritual, love; this paradox is to be found throughout my work.

In the one, individual, woman we see every woman; this is the collective situation in reverse; in the Collective One, primitive man knew, instinctively, every woman; however, these women were but the One, Collective

Woman, in whom all individuals were amassed. In the One Woman, we knew womanhood, in which no woman was distinct; in the individual woman, we do not see indistinct womanhood, *but each, unique, woman in civilisation. Furthermore, in the collective situation primitive man knew—that is, he was aware of though unconsciously— the women by whom he was surrounded, and in whose unity he was immersed; in the civilised situation, man sees—that is, he is consciously aware of—the separate individual women who present themselves to him within his one, unique, sweetheart. Thus we are enabled to remain sexually continent.*

Primitive man and woman are dead, and only potentially alive through their future evolution; civilised men and women are living through their realised evolution (evolution being the journey from 'knowing', or unconsciousness, to 'seeing', or consciousness).

DIVINE LOVE

In the course of this volume, we travel from the dissociation of good and evil, personified by Mother and Whore, to their final reconciliation and transformation in the Ultimate and Absolute Good. The whole saga of good and evil finds its finale in the last section, which reveals once and for all the most intimate details of Christ's life: his passion for, and crucifixion by, his beloved Creation— humanity, in the form of the World Whore.

*   *   *

Throughout this book, when I refer to 'rudeness' I do not mean obscenity, but good, honest vulgarity, without which life would not be worth living. Rudeness, in fact, is but the innermost nakedness, or self-revelation, of the soul.

TO AN AIR STEWARDESS

A Glimpse of an Exquisite, Young Miss

I glimpsed her on a short-haul plane trip to Agadir from Manchester. Never have I been so delighted by the female countenance; I do not know her name, I do not know where she lives, but that little girl—I call her a little girl, though she was the most mature of women—could love the pants off the most egregious letcher—if she had to; for she reserves her love—that superabundance of love— for the one man in her life, never, for one moment, deviating. Smiling sublimely for all passengers, without discrimination, she plies her trade with the solicitude of a little goddess.

But though she is obviously very much in love with

her husband—or boyfriend—she yet has time for me, "Oh, joy! What bliss!" What an honour; she smiled for me, she did not stint her love for me!

That gracious o' so warm, and generous smile— dominates the love-act; she would never eat you alive, as so many hussies would; she would never shag you into a corner: handling you, caressing you, responding, even with fervour, she is never minus that smile. If ever love was proved to be tender, it was in this little gem of womanhood.

(The young lady's name was in fact Helen, as I found out on the return trip.)

*   *   *

Christ himself advocates explicit pleasure, or lust, as contrasted with explicit spirit. God bless that young girl naked in absolute lust, *He loves her,*

We have lust, on the one hand, and spirit on the other—and never the twain shall meet, or so we hope; lust cannot be enjoyed with the interference of spirit; nevertheless it requires spirit in the offing—afar off—to draw it beyond itself to its opposite. The two absolutes need each other, the one to *define and reflect* the other, both together equalling love, the Third Element, which hovers above each, being neither yet both.

While lust is by itself, *it is yet underscored by the*

unconscious awareness of love, which only becomes conscious when lust is drawn beyond itself to spirit, *spirit being conscious love*. Unconscious love and conscious love add up to *love itself*.

There are two kinds of love; spiritual love, and lustful love, which, though they can be experienced together, tend to spoil each other; spiritual love is yet sexual, or erotic, though being biased towards the *platonic* experience of sex, while lustful love is *explicitly* pleasurable or erotic, being concerned with love only unconsciously, but nevertheless definitely. Whichever experience it is, *love itself watches over it, removed yet indulgent*.

Love is always infinitely personal, whether platonic or lustful; we are always aware of the other's nature, however engrossed we are in pleasure; and, even in lust, our principal concern is to give the other pleasure—and that is conscious.

A particular reason for the co-existence of the opposites is that, in the one case, *spirit draws lust up through the body to the heart*—whether or not lust itself remains unconscious of love—thus rendering it innocent; in the other case, lust draws spirit down through the body to the genitals, thus rendering it unconscious and substantiated in pleasure. *Both opposites need each other in every sexual experience*, whether the emphasis is on spiritual, or platonic, love or on explicitly lustful love.

We all need lust, whether combined with spirit or, as

in illicit sex, experienced with a prostitute; a prostitute teaches us the truth of lust in its naked reality. I do not of course condone infantile sexuality, which is dissociated from the innocence of the body as a whole, exaggerated, and confined to the experience of the genitals.

Lust uncomplicated by love is the lost child, common to every prostitute; the prostitute is a legitimate part of every woman, whereby, if she is combined with the loving heart, the prostitute becomes innocent. But because the whore represents the missing part of every woman, she is reviled and cast out; conventional womankind cannot bring itself to acknowledge its illicit sister, the latter needing the former to become innocent, the former needing the latter to find herself.

Being sorely in need of the prostitute, conventional women are always unconsciously susceptible to salacious fantasies, this dichotomy between the conscious and unconscious attitudes being the result of nature's clash with civilization, which causes a fascination with illicit sex; it is my experience that the more consciously virtuous a woman may be, the more likely she is to fall a prey to unconscious depravity, which often comes to the surface. The devil lurks within us all.

* * *

In the experience of explicit pleasure, it is the good spirit, which is otherwise associated with the spirit of giving, remaining therein conscious, that recedes into the background in favour of the 'naughty' spirit; *it is not, in fact, love which is unconscious, but simply the spirit of goodness or virtue*, the absence of which is required so that the essential perniciousness or sportiveness may be allowed full play. Love, after all, in the form of the spirit of giving, is conscious, though we are no longer 'on our best behaviour'.

Love is what determines the conduct, nature, and inspiration, of all sexuality: *we make love by, with, for, and within, love*.

* * *

A prostitute is defined by her all-consuming desire for destruction—not only the desire for her own self-destruction, and the annihilation of any notion of decency, but also for the destruction of God himself and any idea whatever of good. These women are usually either subnormal or abnormal. Prostitution, and the urge for degradation in general, is caused by the woman's personal background, meaning her oppressive, or deprived, upbringing according to parental influence. But where did the attitude of the parents themselves come from? For, ultimately, personal circumstances arise from the overall, disastrous failure inherent in the civilized condition. So if you are looking for the root cause of society's shortcomings, it is to be found in the basic dictation of evolution itself; the burden imposed on us by civilization is caused by the evolutionary programme for the development of consciousness, will, and individuality, brought about by the suppression of Nature upon which civilization is constructed. (There is of course the occasional honourable prostitute.)

CHAPTER I

Sex in General

The idea that sex is for pleasure is a total, and disastrous, illusion.

THE THIRD ELEMENT

The Anglo-Saxon word 'fuck' was originally invented to convey two meanings: one, the process of giving or receiving pleasure, and, two, the expression of spiritual regard, both given and received.

It may not be immediately obvious that spirituality is conveyed in a word that has been synonymous with crudity, but originally—and this has been whispered in my ear—the Anglo-Saxons intended the word to convey the two meanings simultaneously; i.e. as 'Love'. Now, love does indeed consist of both pleasure and spirit; it does not consist of 'sex', which means, specifically, pleasure—usually illicit pleasure—and specifically not spirit. Psychiatrists have been telling us, ever since the end of the nineteenth century, that spirit is a bad thing, because it spoils pleasure. And because psychiatrists are schizophrenics, they are unaware of the dichotomy in their own mentalities; to wit, that if one is asked to make love, or fuck, one needs to employ both spirit and pleasure, because it is impossible to fuck anyone without giving and receiving at the same time: one's cunt and one's cock (two other Anglo-Saxon words) would either not receive any pleasure or not give it, thus rendering the situation into a fiasco, or defeating its original purpose— which is, of course, as Sigmund Freud has tried so hard to convince us, to produce a dirty good shag. Now, a dirty good shag depends specifically on the absence of spirit; pleasure it certainly has, but—and this is where schizophrenia comes in—when both partners are receiving pleasure under such circumstances, it is impossible to determine whether either of them is actually giving it; in point of fact, neither of them is giving it, and it is only received by virtue of auto-erotic self-suggestion—in other words, by illusion; the illusion that one is receiving attention from one's nefarious partner. Apart from the somewhat limited contact between cock and cunt, the two 'partners' are totally divorced, their minds operating in fantasy; and, imprisoned in their own fantastic world, they are unaware of who is shagging whom or whether anyone is actually being shagged anyway. In this twilight world of schizophrenia, therefore, anything goes—and it only 'comes' by dint of much hard pushing and shoving in the locality of the genitals. The result might be considered satisfying, however, if all you are after is a frenetic and dirtily achieved orgasm.

But of course, Dr Psycho maintains that sex was invented for the sole purpose of attaining an orgasm, essentially restricted to the genitals, psychologically, genital-sex knowing no psychological experience, or sensation, in the rest of the body; satisfaction is not felt beyond that frenzied area. So, neither in body nor mind, does illicit sex exist—except, where mind is concerned, in obscene and destructive fantasies which have literally nothing to do with genuine sexuality.

All this can be attributed to the influence of Sigmund Freud—the Father of Sex, but not of Love. Although he recognized the importance of Love in the psyche as a whole, the existence of Love as the purpose and controlling factor of sexuality entirely escaped him. He dissociated sex from Love and presented it as a function independent of those of the rest of the psyche, a conviction supported by G.I. Gurdjieff who, unfortunately for the followers he misled, was governed by his own psychological function of sensation, which in some mentalities does involve the isolation of the 'sex-function'—including its isolation from Love.

Now, God informed me before I came down to earth,

that love is the purpose of sex and that pleasure is the means. It would seem, therefore, that where man is going wrong is in getting things arse-ways about, under the instructions of psychiatry and those who call themselves 'intellectuals'. Of course, man listens to these authorities open-mouthed, not having a mind of his own, though, truth to tell, his mentors haven't any sort of a mind at all. So, then, the blind leading the blind, we are precipitated into a state of mental anarchy whose distinguishing feature is universal Masturbation. Masturbating day and night, on the job or off it, women as well as men, *we live in a world of total fantasy*. Grandmothers and Grandfathers, as long as they can get their leg over, fall into the same category: contained totally within their infantile fantasies, they claw at each other, in their attempts at sexual intercourse, succeeding only in remaining faithful to their adolescent immaturity. Reality they see not—a bum here, a tit there, and a what's-it over there, totally uncombined, totally unintegrated: this is not a body—it is certainly not a mind—it is simply a pre-pubertal glimpse of the chaos within a child's mind—unformed sexuality, pervading society like a rampant disease. This is the civilization wrought upon us by modernism.

Make no mistake about it, love is essential to sex, and not optional, as Dr Psycho pontificates. Thanks to the

Dr's ego-driven, and schizophrenically expressed beliefs, twenty-first century man and woman are perpetually tortured by the schism between lust and love; though this is the age-old problem, it has been exacerbated out of all proportion by psychiatry's unwonted interference. The ignorance of this body, foisted on us by pure conceit, has led us to abandon our birthright of self-respect, specifically recommended on the assumption that sex is intended to be dirty, that we should enjoy it; and the dirtier it is, the more we should enjoy it. Of course, if man could think for himself he would know this is not true, but persuaded by the authority of newspapers and television, who have rallied to Dr Psycho's cause, he lives in the constant conviction that the more he lowers his trousers, the more he is going to enjoy himself—regardless, of course, of his wife's reservations (this, also, being one of the doctor's recommendations). The belief that 'sex is for fun', which flies in the face of God's commands, and also in the face of man's own sense of shame, has prompted society to dedicate itself to the pursuit of evil; where there is no need for restraint, we do not restrain ourselves, and because the overriding purpose of sex is apparently 'to enjoy ourselves', the restraining influence of spirit is not allowed to interfere. And love, the original inspiration and goal of sex—that is, according to God—expires unwanted.

This we see every day, all around us, in the tight-trousered bums and flaunted tits proffered for the express purpose of drawing the dirtiest possible shag. And all because Dr Psycho has told us to do it. The contagion spreads, like flies around shit, from school-room to dance-hall, inspiring the dropping of pants in all directions, in the determination to get that all-consuming orgasm—a seizure of the fanny so pleasurable, apparently, that all sense of decency is frenziedly rejected. Just what the doctor ordered, and in sweaty, frenetic couplings across the land, male and female shag their way into the devil's own Piss-Kitchen.

And they like it because it *is* evil. Innocent pleasure has become evil because of the withdrawal of its tending partner, and *it has developed into the mad desire to destroy even God and Creation itself: rend down those curtains surrounding the Holy of Holies,*

"Just like shitting", as the man said, and this excretory function has been confused with sex, in the mind of man, ever since Sigmund Freud defecated on the idea of natural instinct—which was designed to lead us, mistakenly it seems, to consult our sexual consciences.

Sex is not to be enjoyed.

Pleasure is, of course, love, and love pleasure, as Fanny Hill said; but, as she also added, "love is the only thing that ennobles it". This paradoxical statement is actually very profound—though the lady herself was actually entirely unconscious of that—in that the whole relationship of opposites is essentially one of paradox. Take on board the fact that life itself is Paradox. And from that will ensue our understanding of the meaning of sex.

Right in the heart of pleasure, we find spirit; right in the heart of spirit, we find pleasure; and right in the heart of both of them, we find Love—Love, the king-pin. But think not that the element of spirit is any greater than that of pleasure; *pleasure is, indeed, the purpose of love*; the end to which it is directed and the means by which we achieve it; *while spirit is also the purpose of love*, it is specifically the means by which we are guided through it; without spirit we would be rudderless in the ocean of lust.

Lust, indeed, is actually love—love gone wrong, through the withdrawal of spirit. But it is nevertheless innocent in its origins, being in fact the very inspiration to love: without it, we simply would not want to make love. So, without the desire to shag you, I would not shag you; and you would not have the satisfaction of being shagged.

And shag you, is what I intend to do.

THE IDEAL STATE, AND PURPOSE, OF LOVE...

A Letter Addressed To Venus, My Muse:-

In the determination to love me, she undresses, slowly and deliberately before me, and presents herself, completely naked, for my inspection. Running my eye over her inviting young body, I gulp nervously in contemplation of what I am going to do with her; shall I fuck her straight away, without much circumspection—which she would welcome, as she is now pretty urgent—or shall I prolong her crisis to induce even further pleasure? While I am hesitantly debating my procedure, however, Venus herself decides the matter for me. Lying on her back and signalling her intentions with the most amorous entreaty of her so-beautiful eyes, she parts her lovely thighs, opening herself to me like a flower yearning for the kiss of the sun. And being the gentleman I am, I approach her with all the ardour she has aroused, and enter her, then and there, to prove it. Prone and yielding, the woman I love gives herself up to me, her master, in our mutual rapture.

Thus the abandoned Whore, consecrated by the overwhelming love of the Mother; the one, pleasure itself, the other, pure spirit. Little all the while, little in love—that is how we love each other: "Except ye be as little children, ye shall not enter the kingdom of heaven". And the kingdom of heaven awaits us, not just in our littleness, but also in the magnificence conferred on us by our modesty.

For pleasure is the name of the game, or so I would hope. Most dirty buggars, however, would assume that pleasure is actually the purpose, proceeding on that basis to fuck the living daylights out of her without even an introduction. Now, I myself, being a decent sort of chap, would no doubt fuck the living daylights out of her likewise, but I would generally not omit to introduce myself; for politeness is politeness, and the etiquette of sex has it that you are not allowed to fuck a woman unless you very definitely love her. Pleasure may be pleasure, and thank God for that, but it cannot displace spirit, and most certainly cannot supersede our reason for fucking, which is simply the requirement to barnstorm our beloved into the delirium of Absolute Love—from which there is no return, for, once having been there, Milady has no intention of returning to a mundane world; we hope, therefore that, ideally, her swain will never let her go, but ply her with perfect devotion for the rest of her days—if possible with no relapse into normality.

This is God's design for man. In a constant state of high tumescence, then, the happy couple are expected to remain within love indefinitely; the world may continue around them on its giddy course, but these two have united in a place of Knowledge, issuing from themselves, which will sustain them forever in blissful disregard of earthly cares. Knowledge knows all, and consequently resolves all—which is, on consideration, our ultimate desire.

The passion of pleasure: love given, love received.

There is no hint of disassociation, or exaggeration, in our pleasure. We are Us, and we are Love; that is all. Pleasure, love, and passion: All in One.

And passion is why I fuck you—that word, passion, uniting pleasure with love, and lifting it right out of pleasure into love, thus extinguishing it. *Pleasure must die, so that the spiritual body may live.* And, so transformed, pleasure will yet remain pleasure, but offered to God, and living in God's realm where there is, after all, no pleasure: the Incomprehensible Paradox right at the heart of being.

This knowledge will save all from the ravages of pleasure. Everyone does in fact urgently want to learn about it—even those whores sold to lust. Salvation awaits us all, *because we all want it.*

*   *   *

In that word, 'fuck', I am uniting pleasure with spirit; first of all they were dissociated by having the unity of love withdrawn, which they had initially, and now, after aeons of travail, in which the word 'fuck' became very disreputable, I have established the basis of their future reconciliation—within, again, Love. Love was—Love is. Unity, being disintegrated, now becomes re-integrated in

Union, conscious love ensuing.

Seventy-five per cent of the people in Western Europe are guilty of sexual perversion—a conservative estimate. I do not mean homosexuality or lesbianism, *but the simple fact of downright dirty behaviour.* Whether this is by will or whether involuntary, I do not quite know, but certainly it is wanton and wilful.

Sexual perversion, in this sense of the word, is invariably caused by *dissociation or exaggeration.* When I observe a girl, I don't look at her bum or her tits directly; this would be to dissociate them from the rest of the body, and to exaggerate them at the same time. It is a disgusting, but unfortunately true, fact that most men see only the bum or the tits—*without* the rest of the body; the vast majority of men see a woman as, simply, a bum, a pair of tits, and the crumpet as the focal point: truly a 'sexual object', or objects. How many times have I witnessed this—and it goes without saying that the more a woman omits to wash herself, the better…

Thus the sewer within man's mind in the twenty-first century, to which woman is unwillingly, or willingly, subjected. The focal point of a woman's body is, or should be, the eyes; they are the window of the soul, where the woman lives. Her face, also, reflects her being—not just her other appurtenances, such as the bosom, which is the direct expression of her love, not just her personal being;

the more fulsome a woman's breasts, the more you may be sure of the warmth, or generosity, of her love. Treat her, therefore, with respect. Her bosom is her love, and, its beauty is her loveliness.

Looked at as a whole, woman's body retains its natural integrity, so furnishing her with the dignity which both she and her body deserve. So, gracefully and elegantly, she conducts herself through congress, undressed only to be dressed again in the finer robes of sacred nakedness.

PARSIFAL'S PROPOSITION TO VENUS

My Beloved;

After taking your knickers off, in the most deliberate manner possible, I will proceed to fuck you. Don't be offended, because this Anglo-Saxon word was designed to express love—and it is very effective, especially in conveying what I have in mind for you; which is precisely this: lying you on your back, where you will become shamelessly abandoned to my love—indeed to Love itself—I will force an entry and submit you to a glorious and very satisfying fucking. God put woman on earth to be submissive, but this submission must be prefaced by resistance; though woman wishes all the while to be overcome, man can only exert himself against her if she first resists. Thus the roles of man and woman are defined, and despite the beliefs of 'women's lib' the man is for dominance and the woman is for submission; man leads, woman follows. This has been the inalienable law since history began, and will not be changed by Emily Pankhurst's recalcitrant antics; no person ever did greater harm to the cause of women. If this law did not hold, why would I be fucking you now?

So, on your back—the essential position for all women—you invite me to have my wicked way with you—and by God it is wicked; my designs for you would certainly not be countenanced by the Pope.

Holding you tightly within my arms, so that no harm will ever come to you, I propose to render you into a quivering bundle of joy:

Myself, pushing and shoving within you, and drawing your little heart into mine:

'Come ever nearer to me, my darling, and I will show you the ecstasies of heaven, For, in that little place of yours rests the universe, and God sends to you, there, the knowledge of all'.

You, in ecstasy:

'Fuck me; fuck me, Give me all the ardorous devotion of which you are so capable; and never stop, (if you do, I shall be most frustrated)'.

Myself:

'Closer, closer, Let me stir your innards to the utmost crescendo of life,'

You, in an extreme of urgency:

'Oh, oh, fuck the living daylights out of me!'

So, your passion—as released by me. Caressing you above, and delighting you below, this is how I proceed, bringing heart and body together—I, the Reconciler of all Opposites.

And by combining the needs of both spirit and pleasure we come, ourselves, finally together, breathless after all that hectic effort, yet sublime in our knowledge of each other. In that one, final moment, we witnessed Eternity; we knew the presence of God—adding greatness to our little cause.

But, always proceeding through Love: first, last, and foremost. You can't get a girl's knickers down without approaching her from spirit, first—*in* the act, and *as a result* of the act.

The passion implied in the word 'fuck', which I chose deliberately, is mid-way between spirit and pleasure, being synonymous with love but carrying a slightly different meaning. Passion is the active expression of love, and the act of love determines just that: love. Love being above all, spirit and pleasure, being mere opposites, fade into insignificance. So, the mysterious Third Element, rising between, and above, all its constituent parts—and enveloping them in its all-containing beauty.

You and I know nothing, finally, but the all-consuming passion of Love itself. And so your knickers drop away to reveal only that one thing: the place of Love, and Love alone.

'You and I will fuck forever', you confide in me.—So saying, you lie down on the floor and lift your skirt up, displaying your undying love for me to the world, in your resplendent parts.

We are Love, and Love only. When we are in a high state of pleasure, we are never away from Love; Love is with us, within us, and all around us.

There is so much perverted sex about—that is, dissociated and exaggerated—*that no-one is aware of it*; if you are all in the same boat, the fact that everybody stinks isn't apparent. And this submersion in unconsciousness is deliberate; no-one is prepared to condemn anyone else—a mutually perpetuating confidence-trick whereby, 'If you do not give me away, I will not give you away'. And anyone who breaks this universal law is 'sent to Coventry' for betraying his fellows, which I have personally experienced. Sunk within this inescapable morass, the truth never emerges.

Although people are undoubtedly going to be rabidly aroused against me, I do not anticipate a corporate legal challenge—a few million pigs aren't likely to sue anyone.

The causes of this pathological behaviour are unknown and unreported, and I am here to make them known and to report them.

Unmarried whores, married whores—all are prepared to take their pants off for the purpose of experiencing a dirty bit of fun—as directed by psychology, whether consciously or otherwise; the evil genius of Freud presides over it from beyond the grave—all the more evil for being unwitting. Being faced with the preliminary fact of psychological intervention, all men and women have become convinced, despite their instinctive doubts, that sex is here to stay and had better be enjoyed; that is its evident purpose, and woe betide anyone who goes against the popular trend. No-one, apparently, has the guts to stand up and resist it, preferring to sacrifice his own self-respect on two counts: first, that he is a coward, and second, that he is determined to roll in the shit—for the sake of it. The one God-given fact of all—the isolated gift of self-respect—has been surrendered in the face of physical attack and the desire to commit pure evil—against oneself. Self-respect was set up to combat all attempts to assail the integrity of the Self, in the name of truth, honesty, and the sanctity of life itself; this sanctity is, above all, what is being assaulted. God will not forgive you for that.

So we have lorry drivers selecting their molls for a dirty good screw behind the dustbins, cock-eyed trollops inviting the nearest letcher to rattle their only-too receptive fannies into a dizzy delight, and, in every doorway, mid the complicit shadows, the attempt of the female sex to induce a frantic orgasm by sucking, to the best of their ability, every ounce of sperm from a drunkard's cock.

And yet we have the Archbishop of Canterbury telling us that these women—'working girls', I believe is the term—are actually angels in distress, not responsible for what they are doing—though they can see a man's chopper alright—and that they have become prostitutes for the sole purpose of making money—pleasure, we assume, having nothing to do with it. Far from being forced into their plight—by economic necessity!—These hellions remove their sweaty underwear, all day and all night, purely because they are nymphomaniacs,—Every man's dream, of course—and the sweatier and smellier, the better. The fond illusions of society's do-gooders do not alter the horrific reality of illicit sex—which is not just illicit but actually has nothing to do with sex at all— the very concept is laughable—being the desperate expression of a sickness affecting the whole of civilization. Whores are whores because they feel whoredom where it *is* felt.

This is the wrath of God, speaking.

Upper-class tarts, like Sally and Fanny, are usually the worst, somehow having persuaded the B.B.C. to employ them as 'sex experts'—this term, apparently, conferring social acceptability on what I would have thought was a most unholy calling. Of course, as we know, amateur whores are even more accomplished than their professional sisters. These two representatives of the ruling elite give us the benefit of their extensive experience in demonstrations of how women should dress and behave in order to entrap the opposite sex. 'Stick your bum out as far as possible; walk down the street with the maximum salaciousness—that's right, sway your hips, as if you are trying to catch a fish—and make sure your tits are in full prominence'. All this with the egotistical confidence that they have been chosen to perform an essential service. Their only service is in persuading otherwise innocent women that love is not relevant in sexual affairs, which require only a devotion to an immediate orgasm. And so, orgasmically primed, these unfortunates make their way to their husbands in order to demand attention to their very urgent needs; how they behave on the bus, I don't know.

ORGASM

That little, short-lived moment. Short-lived, did you say? That 'little moment' contains every moment—it lasts for Eternity; all moments in one moment, all time in one moment; realized in the Eternal Present. And we would know—or see—this if we were conscious. So let us become conscious.

One way to do it is to hold back this very, ultimate moment as long as possible—until it hurts; do without it, if you can. Suffering produces consciousness, something which is, or should be, known in the Catholic Church; for celibacy is designed for this purpose; along with its sister goal of Love, Consciousness was the express aim of Popery.

All archbishops, canons, and canonicals will be trained in this venture; for, owing to human susceptibility—as we have seen—priests must learn to master a woman before taking the vow, otherwise they will go wanking and buggaring into the night.

Without the consciousness provided by suffering, how are priests to produce the compassion needed for their 'flock'? How are these potential Parsifals to know, or feel, anything? One moment becomes All moments only through the intervention of divine enlightenment.

As the obverse of the world that God holds in his hand, let that little drop of spunk, emitted by your orgasm, contain everything.

THE CURE

Now to the main purpose of this essay. As you should all know, but don't, I have not come to this earth for nothing; it is my specific duty to clear this farrago of cock-titillators and fanny-rattlers off the face of the earth. God's house will not be used by usurers.

THE SPIRITUAL-BODY

The Twenty-First Century declaration for the evolution of the sexual phenomenon consists of the introduction of the 'Spiritual Body' into man's psyche. This latest dispensation from God will change human sexual behaviour forever—in particular, relieving man of his very nasty erotic habits. Perhaps the most significant thing of all is that the necessity of the act of intercourse itself will be obviated; while the substituted Spiritual Body does not—or need not—involve the sexual act as we know it, it leaves the door open to the sexual experience without the contact of the genitals—though if desirable, this could be included. All options are open.

Pleasure is certainly felt, with or without genital contact; no-one is losing out. The watchword is 'Sublimation'. Man's all-compelling enslavement to the physical side of life—to the very existence of Flesh—is over at one stroke. From now on we are psychological beings.

The psyche—or mind—contains both the body and the mentality; it is a mistake to equate the mentality with the mind, of which it is only a part.

Annie is a very passionate girl. In her we see, on the one hand, her physical passion, on the other, her spiritual passion: the flesh, and the spirit. This most attractive young woman, though not conventionally beautiful, exhibits, more than most, the very unconventional beauty of Emotion; that is to say, her face displays the evidence of a commitment to Passion—the halfway-house between the normal concerns of spirit and flesh. Passion comes from the heart, the location of the true sexual experience, poised mid-way between the genitals and the head, the genitals being ultra-flesh, and the head being ultra-spirit.

Emotion, or Passion, passing through the body—the vessel of Emotion—takes up, from one end, spirit and from the other, flesh, *combining them, within itself, as the Third Element*. This Third Element is the essence of the 'Spiritual Body'.

THE THIRD ELEMENT, THROUGH THE ULTIMATE EXPERIENCE

A little old lady, the other day, stoned out of her mind, offered me the chance to have my chopper cut off free of charge. Now, I know I could get this done on the National Health, but quite frankly, I would prefer her attentions, and of course, the most salubrious scenario would be the receipt of this operation from your own lover, particularly when she is a voluptuous young blonde. In the heat of that very singular moment—your very private parts being severed by your best, and most devoted, friend—indeed, in the most attentively erotic manner possible—surely you would experience the ultimate pleasure? What more could you want from that sacrifice of all sacrifices?

One thing you could want is the metaphysical knowledge of what you were doing. On the one hand we have destruction—the operation—on the other hand we have creation—the orgasm; between the two we have the Schism, assuming there is an unbridgeable gap. If the unbridgeable Schism is to vanish, it must be transformed into a relationship, in other words, into two complementaries, opposites being complementary in an ideal state of relationship. The relationship itself is the Third Element—*including even the Schism.*

But the raw material of all this—the opposites themselves—is the contrast between destruction and creation—two very irreconcilable qualities—yet not so irreconcilable: is not destruction but one remove from creation?—*Are they not identical?* Just as Life and Death fuse into one, under similar circumstances, so destruction—Death—and creation—Life, are finally brought together: the Phoenix of creation rises eternally from the Pyre of destruction, and, ultimately, they know each other in one Pyrotechnical Moment.

Think not that you will get away with identifying spirit with pleasure, or pleasure with spirit; the whole of evolution forbids it. I, in my Second Coming, know all too well the Schism of all things Natural—become, most almightily, unnatural: Natural Man is dead, only to be resurrected in the Union of Opposites—no longer the Unity of former times.

So, take on board the requirements of evolution, and your own psyche. To be, or not to be: that is the thinking question.

Always approach a woman, first, with Love, in which all things are united. But when you shag, you shag with spirit and pleasure first of all separately, then you bring them together—in one, indistinguishable Moment, where pleasure exists separately, but does not exist.

So, the Imponderable Paradox of our human—or divine—nature.

There is no going back to Unity; that is now denied us,

forbidden us; which is why Buddhism is in such a parlous state—indeed, a time-warp. Christianity holds the way forward, into the future—Union—born of a desirable, though necessarily disastrous, Duality—a real Duality. Dualism may have its drawbacks, as has plurality, but they both exist, and have a right and purpose in existing. The fact that plurality is inconvenient for Buddhist thought does not mean it is an illusion—unless you consider that the whole of the exterior world is an illusion (which I can prove is not the case). Where Buddhists go wrong is in equating the exterior world with the physical world—an understandable problem in the light of their centrifugal psyche.

In place of 'Christian', I would put forward the name 'Antonian'—meaning the 'Antonian' religion, as I do not espouse, beyond a certain extent, the Christian religion itself; the Antonian is built upon the relics of the Christian religion, with smatterings of every other religion thrown in as well. This should mollify any residual egotism lurking around the world.

[Without spirit, we would have not the pleasure; without pleasure, we would have not the spirit].

[We do not desire each other's' bodies; we desire each other].

Returning to the 'Spiritual-Body':-

Much as I regret my debarment from the indulgence of physical desire, *this can all be sublimated in the emotional state*: a compromise between, and a combination of, spirit and body—resolved in the Heart. The heart is where Christ proposes to conduct his programme for the world—essentially through *imagination*; a process which at the moment only Christ can produce. Imagination, as Christ is putting it forward, is a vastly different thing to the so-called 'imagination' present in the conventional idea. I have come here to revolutionize all conventions and concepts, imagination being one of them. Imagination, therefore, is a free-ranging ability to 'see all'; imagination sees everything. ('Free-ranging' is a very adequate, Jungian phrase.) This is what the faculty always has consisted of, but has remained unrecognized until now. It also contains reason, contrary to all accepted belief.

Imaginative thinking is the way forward for the modern world—perhaps Christ's most valuable gift. In it is resolved the whole question of the inner and outer lives, these being brought together in the Spiritual-Body: a combination of subjective and objective factors, *which relieves one of the necessity of living and working within the physical body*, unless one chooses to do so—in other words, among other things, one is able to make love conducted on an emotional though not physical, basis, *mid-way between body and spirit: including both, but, essentially, not of both.*

[See 'Sublimation', from the preface to *The Knowledge of Everything*; also 'Transubstantiation' from the essay,

'Sudanese Blasphemy Crisis' (*Knowledge of Everything*); also 'Secret of Desire', again from *Knowledge of Everything*.]

*   *   *

AN AMOROUS FROLIC

The creasing of the upper thigh,
Under the welt of a black stocking—
The swelling, strategic areas
Beneath a nice, black nègligée—
The endearing and fervent scent
Of a woman in her amorous embrace:
These things, so intimate,
Are not to be forgotten.
Abandoning the nègligée,
She clasps her hands behind her head,
Offering her full-bosomed self to my regard,
And, shifting her hips—not her backside—
Slightly, she disposes herself
In a more inviting position;
What more could a man stand?
Such response this brings,
That I am moved to a sturdy vigour
In those regions below the belt;

And what more could a ladies' champion do
Than take advantage of a very critical situation.
Inspired to an ardent clinch, therefore,
We enjoy the ecstatic mode
Of Love's transporting ways

*   *   *

[Masturbation, pervades all aspects of life.]

[Woman is born whole, and so she doesn't need to travel through the journey of masturbation to become mature.]

*   *   *

Teenage boys must 'masturbate' (to use a nasty term) for a long time before they can achieve sexual maturity. 'Making love to your hand', therefore, is a necessary and indispensable preliminary to making love to your later sweetheart—who will not despise you for it—especially when it produces such beautiful experiences for herself,

So let us go wanking.

A NOTE ON THE COSMIC PHYSIOLOGY OF SEXUALITY

You and I experience the knowledge of each other in that conveyancing medium called 'pleasure'. Pleasure is designed for the express purpose of enabling us to know each other in and through love. In itself, pleasure does not exist, on the basis that it represents, quintessentially, the illusion of the physical world, being used for the purpose of love, and that is all; the physical world is set up to facilitate intercourse between the opposites, after which it retires, redundant, and vanishes into the ether from which it came.

Nevertheless, I can only know you, I can only give you love, through that febrile tissue of pleasure; so it is extremely useful, but as all functions, it has no other reality except as the function it actually is, limited to itself and shortly to be deprived of its existence when viewed through the all-seeing eye of consciousness—the product of love.

Let us honour pleasure, therefore, but let us not make it a god.

Desire being passion, we find ourselves committed to pleasure: why else would you desire to be fucked? (the word, fuck, being much more beautiful than the derogatory term of shag). Being so passionate in your experience of pleasure (why else would I love you?) you force me to acknowledge the very sanguine fact that pleasure, far from being restricted to the genitals, extends over the whole body and particularly into the mind— where it comes from. Being felt, perhaps, most intensely in the genitals, the sheer joy, the passion of pleasure originates within the mind, and proceeds from it, reverberating around your rapturous body, and, only as a last resort, penetrating to the genitals; the focal point, however, is not in this transient area but in the eyes. The eyes reflect the music of the soul or mind: *the pleasure centre*; from where it proceeds again around the body and returns to the mind, and back eternally, on its constant round, increasing in intensity as it goes. This climactic journey is facilitated, at each of its stations, by the transforming spirit of libido, which effects the necessary paradox, turning spirit into pleasure and back again. Without this constant transformation, the opposites would become fixated in their own exaggerated and isolated position—hence resulting in the pathological paralysis which we know as 'perversion'—a condition which affects most people in Western civilization—which perpetuates, by its paralyzing influence, its fatal, fantastic illusion, reducing even intercourse to the permanent immaturity of masturbation. Masturbation remains in most of us until death.

Where is this Centre, the Soul? Is it in the head? Is it in the heart? Is it in the body? Or is it in the genitals? It is in all these places, and far beyond them, emanating from the outer reaches of the universe—*and at the same time, from the very centre of it.* This is the experience of God: the source of all pleasure and passion—combined at once in Love, the true purpose, and sole justification for, *a pleasure that, finally, does not even exist,* having played a yet noble part in the creation of the greatest climax known to the life of us humans.

So, therefore, do not decry pleasure—nor, if you are a psychiatrist, the opposite, spirit. Taken together these two form not just the basis of love, *but the foundation of all knowledge*: the knowledge of Good and Evil, the observation of Essence and Existence, forming between them the ultimate consciousness of Metaphysics. This hybrid method of knowing and seeing is the goal of our existence, furnishing us by its very function with the means of finding it: the Paradox which draws us on through the daylight of Masculinity into the mysterious night of the Feminine.

And thus, all men and women come together in the celebration of Eternal Life upon earth.

* * *

Only by will can we reverse the deadly influence of masturbation; only by taking upon ourselves the lengthy journey of maturation do we stand any chance of freeing ourselves from its stranglehold. *The application of will for this purpose requires prolonged consciousness, that in itself being acquired only by painstaking experience in the very maturation process.* Consciousness confers knowledge; knowledge cures.

We have to come to know ourselves, through honesty and the attempt to abandon ego, ego being the very thing which blinds us to reality—even the reality of sex. Without coming to know ourselves, and consequently our sexual nature, sexuality will never develop, and we will be left behind in our masturbatory prison. The one thing, above all, which qualifies maturity, is Love. Without love, woman would not make love to man, nor man to woman; the expression is 'making love', not 'making sex', and the attempt to substitute sex for love lies at the bottom of that monstrous evil called 'modernism', unleashed on us by, among others, Pankhurst and Freud. Freud ended love itself, Pankhurst ended femininity—the very quality needed most in love, by both women and men. Loveless, the twentieth century proceeded with the clarion cry, 'We do not need woman, we do not need God!' Both God and woman died on the cross of modernist untruth; and love died with them.

*   *   *

ANGELA BROWN

This example of perverted womanhood has bestridden the stage of modern sexuality for nigh on fifty years (she looks old enough, anyway). Lined and be-wrinkled, yet still thinking herself young enough to invite the whole male sex into bed with her, she holds forth in the media as the champion of sex-without-love. This is her manifesto: 'Shag all and everything', without a care in the world—why should you have?—you're not committed to anybody. That would defeat the purpose of it, anyway, which appears to be to demonstrate the deliberate extirpation, not just of spirit, but also of any personal connotation whatever.

Without the person to do the shagging, no shag can take place, and in place of the shag we are left with, of course, masturbation. This, in all but name, is what she seeks; the withdrawal of personal involvement leaves the sex act without a focal point—or a purpose; the classic case of adolescent self-abuse.

So we are left with the schizophrenic identity of, on the one hand, an ignoramus masquerading as an intellectual, and on the other, a man masquerading as a woman.

The 'Feminist Movement' having actually removed all traces of femininity from women in general and from the act of love in particular, we are minus the precious influence of the feminine; there is no womanhood, and consequently no love, and no civilization either. For civilization is built on Love and the Feminine Principle. These are the consequences of Emily Pankhurst's exhibitionist tendencies. And, in passing, there has never been a convincing case made out for the right of women to vote, 'Why should men have the exclusive right to vote? This is unfair to women'. For anything to be unfair to women, you have first to prove that women are on an equal footing to men; Nature invented women with the express intention of their being inferior. Men, by design have always been the leaders, and, in my opinion, this does not make women actually inferior: they would only appear so as the result of Pankhurst's interference, upon which the ugly head of ego reared itself. Previously, Nature had managed to ensure that woman had no ego; that salutary fact had sustained woman throughout evolution, and, by God's purpose as well as Nature's, man was very often restrained from going to war on this same account. Woman's lack of ego has enabled her to counsel her opposite sex on matters so grave as aggression and sexuality, and it is the purpose of evolution to create civilization on the very basis of man's adoption of the feminine trait. Thus, if you subtract femininity from civilization, we revert to savagery. And the primitive savage we see today in the person of woman—demanding everything, from the right to work to the right to do away with their unborn child—was created by the declaration that women should assert themselves in the role of men, quite contrary to their nature.

It is an undoubted fact also, that, in contradiction to his natural tendencies, man has succumbed to the very quality that made civilization possible: the feminine trait. So effeminate is Western man at this moment, that our civilization will not survive an attack from the Muslim East, the Muslim religion never having attempted to force femininity on its own people. Whether you consider this to be a good thing or not, it has enabled the Muslims to defeat every Christian effort to overcome them from the Crusades onward. As the Arabs constantly point out to me, on looking at Western culture, the women are all like men, and the men are all like women; which has a distinct advantage, I suppose, in the event of attack, where men will cower in the kitchen while the women go forth sword in hand—and God help those bloody Muslims,

I have come here to teach the British nation to fight, and the first thing I am going to do is to get hold of every vicar and archbishop in the land and set them up in the ring with boxing gloves on. I'll have them fighting like heroes—and I'll throw in a few psychiatrists as well. God never told womankind to don their husbands' trousers; unfortunately, Mrs Thatcher thought he did, and as a result we were treated to the unwelcome spectacle of this redoubtable woman taking on the Russians on behalf of the vacillating British male. If my Father had come out of retirement, he would have married that woman, and he would have proceeded to tame her by taking her pants down and smacking her little bottom. Femininity having thus been restored, the happy couple would have retreated to a bungalow in Blackpool, where we would never have heard from her again—but we'd have lost a good prime minister.

All women need to be beaten, and any impertinent challenge to their husband's authority must be put down. Man rules, woman obeys—the natural law ever since Christ last bestrode the earth. All you modern pansies be warned: a woman does not respect a man if he respects her; the greatest respect a man can show a woman is *not* to respect her. Woman needs to be taken, not asked—if, that is, she is a natural woman, and hasn't been subverted by Pankhurst's disastrous attentions. I have fucked thousands of women into the experience of heaven— precisely because I forced them. They wanted to be fucked, of course, but they wouldn't submit unless they were sure that their lover intended to dominate them; the very resistance they put up is intended to be overcome.

The rôles of men and women have been reversed, and despite the beliefs of the church and Mary Whitehouse, God did not intend this change of gender in his virile world. The Archbishop of Canterbury's skirt hides a meagre pair of testicles.

Women have no business, either, being nuns. Nuns invariably reek of decaying flesh; as they have never been fucked, their bodies have gone rancid, and being therefore unnourished, they stink; God does not welcome a malodorous female in his bed. The 'Brides of Christ' are rejected.

Men and women are put on earth for only two purposes: to fight and to fuck; but I wouldn't fuck a nun if I was paid to. They are not even allowed to look at their own fannies,

AN EARLY LOVE AFFAIR

(I address all those who have accused me of lust.)

When I first saw E, I thought, 'Fuck me, now there's a frustrated woman!' Frustrated through love, not sex; I knew that from the start. Her husband was an impotent old goat who had subjected her to starvation for thirty years; when I reached her she was fifty, still with a lovely, though severe, face and with the miraculously-preserved figure of Aphrodite. So modest was she that she would not be photographed in her bathing suit, a one-piece garment that served to conceal her very considerable charms from the prying eye, and perhaps she was reluctant to be photographed, also, because the sexual implications were so important to her: she would not let this secret out of the bag to anyone. Though rejected by her husband, she still retained her womanly commitment to him as the only possible man in her life, and therefore she would not let anyone see her plight, or the charms she still reserved for him.

Every day, I saw this woman, whom I adored—and loved more, even, than my own self—driven to an emotional crisis which usually resulted in a migraine-attack; this was her daily régime. Her husband, a doctor, was forced to inject her, daily, with some drug designed to relieve her extremity; it was not very effective. But this injection, delivered quite high up on the thigh was the only intimacy, or love, that E received from her husband, and so she welcomed his attentions.

While she was in this desperate condition, I first came to live in E's home. So, desperate myself with love for her, I knew I had to take some action.

Walking in the woods one day, we stopped by a gate; E was looking, in an abstracted fashion, into the distance, with myself standing beside her. Whether I knew the implications of what I was doing, I don't remember, but I was determined to show her somehow what I felt for her; so I very gently and circumspectly placed my hand on the small of her back. Now, that is a highly significant place, as I knew; for it is mid-way between the heart and the body—that is to say, the business-end of the body—and therefore indicated love and physical passion combined. By my action, therefore, I was saying, 'I love you more than anything in the world; if you are willing to let me take you, I will, but I would not force you under any circumstances'. This certainly got through to her, but I was not sure how conscious she was of it; unconsciously she was very well aware of it, and she knew my intentions from then on. She did not reject me, but I soon withdrew my hand, respecting her enough to be prepared for a lengthy courtship.

Once, in an attempt to tell E of my identity, in response to her remorseful complaint that she was too old for me, I said to her, 'You are as young as the day you were born, And I am as old as Eternity'.

Reluctantly she replied, 'You're quite a poetic boy, aren't you?' My first poetic sally had met with a lukewarm reception, and my identity certainly remained in doubt.

On another, most singular, occasion, she told me that when she passed her old family home, after half a lifetime's absence, she suddenly burst into tears; obviously she had been overwhelmed by memories of a once roseate and happy childhood…

LOVE'S WAY

One afternoon, after a flaming row—caused, probably, by my own fear that she did not love me—she ran off into the sitting-room in tears, crying: 'How can you say that to the woman who worships you?'

She had always been in the habit, when feeling particularly unhappy—which was frequently—of sitting down at her beloved piano and playing her favourite, and usually heart-rending, tunes. Realizing the enormity of what I had done, I hastened to her and, loving this woman with all the unreserved passion which only I know, I approached her from behind, my own tears flowing copiously, and very tenderly placed my hands over her breasts. I knew very well what would follow. She rose immediately, and, tears ceasing, she took me by the hand and guided me to the sofa, where both of us had every intention of expressing our long-pent-up feelings. And so we did. She took off her skirt, and lay back over my knees, in abandonment to my love; this was a woman who, though never having experienced love before, knew just what to do—and she had the right man to do it.

Unfortunately, I was not able to have intercourse with her (a lifetime's forbearance). So I did the only thing I could do, and pushed my hand up her pants; as I couldn't immediately find her Intimacy, she whispered, 'Further forward'. So I entered her, with my hand, and in the determination to give her the utmost pleasure, I shoved it right up as far as I could—right up to the top of her little womb. The effect was immediate and devastating. How could so uniquely responsive a woman resist such a thing— the one and only fantastic orgasm she had ever received; there, in my arms, her lifelong frustration was released.

It was the first time in her life she had received any pleasure—and certainly any love. And so intensely did I love her that, when I withdrew my hand I placed it in my mouth, receiving the remaining evidence of her passion. This was the *ultimate demonstration*, to E, of my love, not causing me, in any way, a thrill or pleasurable sensation. Surely such overwhelming commitment to a woman was never witnessed?—Demonstrating finally, to her, that this was not pleasure, but God's love, come down to earth for *her*. And in love, nothing is forbidden, and nothing is shocking. Anyone who thinks this was not love, has my fist to deal with.

And so, even at that tender age, though it was the first time I had ever made love to a woman, I knew so well how to do it: an expert in love, guided by love itself.

There was a practice at that time, in both America and over here, between couples who wished to make love before marriage, without spoiling it by actual intercourse, of comforting each other by hand. It was on this basis that our affair was conducted, because never, during the whole course of my life, have I permitted myself the ultimate knowledge of woman, reserving this for the one woman who, towards the end was apparently able to call it forth from me: her right to do so, and my right to respond. Not even E succeeded in drawing this out.

My affair with E lasted only a year, because, knowing, after all, that she belonged to another man, and that I was knocking her off in his own house, I was forced to terminate it out of respect for him.

After I had gone, she never knew love again.

I have remained silent all these years in consideration for her family; I ask them to forgive me for my relations with their Mother.

This is the truth about my 'dirty' liaison.

BUT DARKNESS DESCENDED

This is the terrible thing: E, the most innocent woman in the world—the one, above all, most capable of love— was led, by these very qualities, into the clutches of whoredom. Owing to a lifetime of denial, and total absence of any nourishment whatever, her very capacity for love was starved into the expression of its very opposite; her desperation resulted in hatred—hatred probably directed at her husband originally, but turned inwards on herself. For without the ability to project your feelings onto the one you love—because it would destroy them—you have no recourse but to destroy yourself. And so E's boundless love for her husband became converted into the consumptive passion of a whore.

Yes, those two extreme qualities can be combined in the same person; how many times have I observed this? So it was with dismay that I saw this happening. Without going into distressing detail, I will just say that, long before I got to E, she had been destroyed—perverted, in fact; this remained unconscious to herself—and to me— until, several times, it was revealed in her 'less spiritual' approaches to me. I have, unfortunately with frequency, been witness to the appalling paradox right at the heart of woman's nature: the Whore co-exists with the Mother; the former unconscious, the latter, conscious.

In a woman's normal life, assuming she hasn't been seduced either by herself or by somebody else, the Whore and the Mother work together harmoniously; the one complements the other; pleasure itself, the Whore, works together with spirit itself, the Mother—to produce Love, the over-arching Third Element. Love consists of the combination of pleasure and spirit, *and as long as both of them remain within Love, they retain their innocence*. But once they step outside Love, they automatically lose that innocence; they become dissociated—dissociated from each other, and from Love itself. In a case of sensational sex, which is a comparatively rare occurrence, innocence is maintained by the presence of both opposites—spirit and pleasure—even though Love itself may not be present. This situation is only possible through the existence of Unity, *the unconscious condition in which the opposites, spirit and pleasure, are unified, or in identification.* In this state of identification, the opposites are totally innocent—*because no-one can tell the difference between them: the Knowledge of Good and Evil—or consciousness—has not set in*. This womb of unconsciousness is the birthplace of Adam and Eve—innocent man and woman, both possessed of the indistinguishable opposites; we have, on the one hand, Adam—the Father and the Rake—and on the other, Eve—the Mother and the Whore. But when Eve eats the apple—*offered not by the serpent, but by God himself—for this is his design for humanity*—lo-and-behold, all hell breaks loose. Eve and Adam saw that they were naked; Eve looked at her fanny, and Adam looked at his chopper, and together they exclaimed, 'We are evil; what will the Lord think of us?' But the Lord shook his head, and said, 'Think not that you are evil, think not that you are good: *think both together, at once'*.

At one stroke, the situation is restored. Innocence returns to Adam and Eve, the Knowledge of Good and Evil receives its twenty-first century update, and everything from now on will be hunky-dory,—Providing you accept Christ—sorry, Anthony Hill—a most unlikely name, which isn't even aristocratic—but in the guise of this much-persecuted lunatic, Jesus has come again to teach you—and to take away your ego.

Removing the ego of every man, woman and child entails the restoration of innocence to the psyche as a whole. One of the ego's most negative contents is masturbatory fantasies; now, whether you are a teenager or a supposedly grown man or woman, you will be subject to fantasies on two levels; first, sexual fantasies, and second, self-aggrandizing fantasies—both of which add up to self-love, or ego itself; so if you dismiss ego, you dismiss self-love, and consequently masturbation and self-aggrandizement as well. Quite an achievement, and worth doing, because if you *don't* dismiss these egoic qualities, you are left without innocence, maturity and love; in other words, you remain an evil man. The greatest evil is self-deception, brought about by self-love. Love must be turned outward, away from the self, and by thus attaining maturity, we do away with masturbation on all levels.

Masturbation, a horrible word—Dr Johnson should have known better—is defined in two ways: self-abuse, and auto-eroticism; imprisoned in his, or her, fantasies, the masturbator flogs his tom or, in the case of a woman, rubs her fanny, day and night in an attempt to imprison the opposite sex with him in his own mind. Even in the role of a rapist or paedophile, actually engaged on the job, the masturbator doesn't know who he is fucking or whether he is fucking at all. The solitary masturbator, tucked up in his stinking bed, doesn't actually try to abuse another person, thereby becoming a criminal, but he does abuse himself *by committing the cardinal sin of self-deception.* Whatever else we do, we mustn't do that: God says, if we are going to do any fucking, we must fuck the real thing; a sensible recommendation, because if we don't fuck the real thing, how are we to make babies and perpetuate the human race? A point to consider, remembering that God also told us, I believe in the Bible, to 'go forth and multiply,' Darwin took up the cry, though I think he rather missed the point as usual, by telling us that fucking was for the specific purpose of procreation. Now I don't agree with that, and nor does God; God once imparted to me, in one of our nightly conversations, that man was put on earth to love; procreation is all very well, and very necessary, but Darwin was customarily concerned with the reduction of all life, love and learning to the one factor of Function. Unfortunately that definition remains with us today, and the chief legacy of 'Darwinian Evolution' is twofold: we all go around shagging like rabbits, convinced that there is no such thing as love, and, if there were, there shouldn't be, and everyone, despite his initial disgust, receives with alacrity his wife's well-meant farts projected from the anal-presentation position. This is on the recommendation of Darwin's devoted follower, Dr W, who informs us that love or in his case, sex, should be performed on the basis of Smell. His conclusion, apparently, results from his observation of the sexual antics of apes with diarrhoea: what better smell could you get than that? He went so far as to demonstrate his findings with clinical tests. One further note:- it emerges from the mists of the nineteenth century, a particularly backward era, that one of Darwin's colleagues, possibly Nietzsche, has apparently subtracted God from the universe; now, last time I saw him, about six months ago, the old boy was still alive and kicking, and he will be most surprised to learn that he is dead.

There is a grey area between the conscious and unconscious, generally known as the 'sub-conscious'; this is where the transactions between the unconscious, or Instinct, and the conscious, or Ego, take place; *obviously a very important area, and the relationship between Ego and Instinct has to be maintained, otherwise Ego becomes egotism.*

The Ego itself is simply the area of consciousness: the consciousness of Self, or I. The normal consciousness of Self enables us to lead a civilized and harmonious life; although the Self actually includes the whole of the psyche, apart from the very grey area at the bottom of Instinct, where it is joined to the Universal Psyche, the actual consciousness of Self, or 'self-consciousness', is basically restricted to the egoic area. The remaining 'awareness' of self, probably moving to 'self-respect' in this regard, is essentially unconscious, manifesting itself emotionally.

It is this area, or aspect, of the psyche which has been under threat from psychology for over one hundred years; the very discipline set up to defend the mind's integrity, is responsible for its demise. This loss of self-respect, giving way to self-love, breaks up not just the sanctity of the psyche but also its wholeness.

THE CHEMIST'S SHOP

A girl I had known for some time, came to me one day and demanded that I love her. She and I had always 'felt' for each other. She was very warm and attractive, despite the fact that she wasn't obviously beautiful, and had a caste in one eye; but she was one of those unfortunate souls who had never found solace in her husband; now it was time I did something about it.

And so I made love to her—right there, on the spot, in that very chemist's shop.

We embraced. Taking her knickers down (always a prerequisite) without any circumspection whatever, I resolved to give her, once and for all, such love and passion as only Christ is capable of—with the greatest possible pleasure. With all my abundant masculinity, I reduced her to a fullness of swooning delight, and we eventually came to each other so closely that we didn't know who was whom.

'You darling, wonderful girl,' I managed to impart:

'You darling, wonderful man,' she whispered, just as she went under.

And I went with her, of course: that was the whole point of it.

Half an hour later, duty done, I said goodbye to her: 'You know, don't you, that this can never happen again? You have to go back to your husband'. 'Yes, I know'.

*　　*　　*

There is as much of a lobby against pleasure as for it. I favour neither point of view, but both.

*　　*　　*

Not only is pleasure an illusion, *but sex itself is an illusion*, sex being pleasure. The whole concept of 'sex'—and that means, expressly, not love—was born, latterly, of the late nineteenth-century notion that humans are naturally pigs; that is the unspoken, and underlying, implication if not the conscious admission. Darwin was almost singlehandedly responsible for it, his theory, 'The Origin Of Species', serving only to prove that, right at the beginning of Creation, there was, in God's mind, the design to separate out the psychological functions. Where Darwin went wrong was in deciding that everything in evolution *was physical*; he acknowledges the existence of mind—presumably—but this has, apparently, no bearing on the serious conduct of life, being merely a bloody nuisance when we are attempting to prove the non-existence of God. God will take a lot of convincing that he is defunct. However, if Darwin says so, He is, and He cannot argue with that.

Consequently, if God has died, his values, presumably, have died with him. And that is precisely what has happened. God's two chief purposes for man—to Love and to Learn—have been dismissed by Darwin as 'old hat' and when you say something is 'old hat' it gives carte-blanche to people like Pankhurst and Freud to follow suit. Unable to think on their own account, they take up the prevailing trend and, through the only quality they do possess—unbounded conceit—they blithely assert that, God being dead, us humans can do what we like: no-one to punish us—the very thought would be criminal. Hence, 'Human Rights', the 'Declaration of the Rights of Man', the 'Rights of Woman', and just about every 'right' left in the book—*except the right to Self-Respect.*

On Self-Respect hangs every value God has vouchsafed us; from Love to Learning, to the Pursuit of Happiness—which comes about through the other two. We may be entitled to pursue happiness, but we have no inalienable right to happiness itself, which, if we ever do attain it, depends on our own efforts and not on God's bounty. In the pursuit of happiness, then, the first requirement of ourselves is Self-Respect. Self-respect is demanded of us by God, and presented to us by God. The First Law—not the First Right—is, 'Citizen, respect thyself'. Through this Divine Ordination, we are enabled to proceed through life, distributing bountifulness wherever we go and charity to all and sundry, in the knowledge within our souls that anything you or I may do depends ultimately on one thing—*the contract between God and man: each to respect the other, and man to respect himself.*

Not even the Pope has the right to wank in public; only the Son of God can do that. And he would do it *out of his own perverted self-respect, which leads him, through love, to destroy himself—on a public cross*. You see the Son of Man in his extremity: to be or not to be.

For, by being himself, he is forced to condemn man; and rather than condemn the very thing he loves most, he chooses to condemn himself, and ends up in life-long, self-crucifixion. Such is Christ's disgust with himself, at his own duty, that he wallows in the shit of the sewers rather than pick himself up and become the Slayer of Man's Ego. Such an access of madness is incomprehensible, unless you consider Christ's incredible love for His own world, and for that wretch, man, whom He created out of His own sweat and blood.

Thus crucified, he continues today.

As we were saying, upon the withdrawal of his self-respect—something subtracted by Darwin's authority—man has evolved since the nineteenth century on a course of destruction and self-degradation—for much the same reasons as Christ, except that He was inspired by His own will, whereas man in his weakness follows the common herd. This respect for ourselves is required to be abandoned by the tenets of the *Origin of Species*, whether Darwin realized the implications or not, and today the situation is so extreme that, on every street-corner we see prostitutes trading their wares, and drug-addicts plying their needles. Masturbation is rife across the board—and not just in the instance of sex; in the illusion of existence itself we see reflected the illusions of every man jack of us.

Just as existence as a whole is a vast illusion, so physicality, *including the body itself*, is also a fundamental chimera; sex, pleasure, and the whole carnal gamut are beyond the pale of any reality whatever, the only semblance they might have had being spurted into nowhere by the ejaculations of an equally spurious masturbatory fantasy.

The overwhelming superiority of the mind over the body means that the body accounts for only one per cent of the reality of sexuality, the further ninety-nine per cent being reserved for the mind. The heart itself probably accounts for one hundred per cent of the mind in any sexual experience; consequently, it is impossible to approach a woman sexually except through Love, conducting the whole experience, furthermore, on the *basis* of Love.

* * *

THE FEMALE GENITALS

Holiest of Holies, Mystery of Mysteries—so the female cunt, and all its attendant foliage; woman's most welcoming intimacy—an invitation, to man, of the utmost privilege.

Seen objectively, neither the female nor the male genitals might possess the utmost beauty; but beauty is in the eye of the beholder—or in the eye of the lover. And seen objectively, again—in other words, as an object—the pubic hair is automatically dissociated from the rest of the body, from which it would receive its true identity and aesthetic acceptance.

I would die for the honour of approaching such a threshold, being drawn from the ends of the earth to this sacred, mystical shrine.

When I observe a woman's hips—not her backside—I see them in the context of the whole body; that way, they aren't exaggerated or dissociated. I glance from the corner of my eye, so as not to look directly—which would be another insult to her.

TO VENUS

I am going to induce in you the utmost possible pleasure—

for you, in you, with you.

I will raise your passion to its highest and most

ecstatic expression;

I know how to do it. I will do it.

With the greatest attention to detail,

in every possible way,

I will deliberately transport you into the
most extreme orgasm

You could possibly imagine or receive.

And you will love me so much

that you will cry out in your very passion—

right then and there—on the spot—

absolutely abandoned to the will of your Master.

And so you, my Mistress,

Having called forth my unfailing requite,

will then rapturously relax in the afterglow

of a fantastic experience,

your face suffused with a lovely pink flush,

And your eyes regarding me, in their delighted

mistness,

With all the love which only a woman like you

can offer me.

*   *   *

And if anyone asks you, 'was this pleasure?' you can
confidently answer them, 'No, this was Love'.

NOTE TO ALL TEENAGERS:
WHY YOU CAN'T MAKE LOVE

The reason you can't make love is that you are a mangy

juvenile; you are immature: that is why you are a teenager. Teenagers cannot have sexual intercourse because they have not grown up yet; the ability to achieve an orgasm is not an indication of man's estate. They haven't climbed out of the cradle yet, and don't know whether to put it in her ear or up her arse, which is the main reason why most girls don't get pregnant. If you were to put it up her vagina, you would ring the bell at once; consequently it is only the more intelligent who get pregnant—which isn't saying much. The rest of you are certainly wise enough to avoid the complications of love—if you know what that means.

But the complications of love, and growing up in general, are something you are unable to grasp; teenagers are not designed to make love until they have reached the stage of adulthood, and, while they are still in their nappies, which is usually until the age of eighteen or so, they are obliged to masturbate.

Wanking is the name of the game, and you must continue to wank yourselves silly until you are man enough to Love. For only Love will save you. And sex is made not *with* Love, but *for* Love, and *by* Love, and *within* Love.

Remember that, all ye would-be Lotharios.

CHAPTER II

The Universal Sexual Psychosis

Only love has the power to awaken sexuality.

The pathological condition of sexuality affects both East and West.

First of all, let me say that it could be cut short simply by the substitution of love for lust. But the deplorable immaturity of man dictates that lust should rule him universally and absolutely.

In the West, the main catalyst to lust was Sigmund Freud, whose legacy has been adequately upheld by his psychiatric progeny. There is no love left in sex. Emily Pankhurst's contribution was to subtract femininity from woman's make-up, with the identical result that love, also, was withdrawn from woman as well as from sex. The feminine element is what enables both women *and* men to love. What we are left with is two mutually-destructive swine.

The only manner in which. intercourse can be conducted within this resulting condition of blind lechery, is through masturbation—mutually, and totally, illusionary. You simply are not having intercourse with the person in front of you.[1]

The only reality is love, to which the physical world must die—and that includes physical pleasure. If you want to treat a woman with honour, *first of all sacrifice your lust, until you find it again within love.* For lust is hallowed by love, and finds itself in its right place—"the same but different"—transformed by love itself.

The situation in the East is basically different to that in the West. In the West, our culture is inimical to Nature, or the natural instincts, and our psychosis is largely a result of the attempt to subdue Nature (which we are required to do in the Bible). In the East where relations with Nature are harmonious, the psychosis derives from the *unleashing* of Nature—where it isn't *meant* to be unleashed. Of course, it isn't Nature that is released, but man's lust. In both hemispheres there are 'clean-living' people, but the majority, in the West, are perverted, while, in the East, many, also, are perverted. It is no surprise that Eastern—and Western—fundamentalism is largely concerned with sexual license.

It is no excuse to plead that you *combine* sex with love, or experience it as an *otherwise* loving relationship. Sex *is* love; as Fanny Hill says, "Pleasure is love, and love

1. Obviously I am not talking about handling your own self for an orgasm.

pleasure—and love the only thing that ennobles it". This paradox has to be understood. One makes love *by* love, *for* love, and *within* love—not *with* love, or *besides* love. Love is not optional. While the *idea* of pleasure may be *separated* from love, in order to be consciously examined, *pleasure should never be experienced outside love*. It is only as an idea that pleasure exists; the world of physical experience is, as I have demonstrated many times, a complete illusion, its only reality taking place within love—the great transforming power, where exists Paradox par excellence.

When she says, "Love is pleasure, and pleasure love", she is indicating the opposites; when she adds, "and love the only thing that ennobles it", she is actually adding the Third Element, or Love itself, which, while incorporating the opposites within itself, yet soars far above them. (Where Fanny makes her mistake is in equating one of the opposites, spirit, with Love, which, while it has much in common, is far superior. As opposites, spirit and pleasure are mere terms, or dots within the infinity of the Cosmos.)

On reading the *Kama Sutra* and other Indian, or Eastern, manuals on love—or, rather, sex—I am left with the impression that, not once, is the word 'love' mentioned. Allowing for the fact that, in the East, the original state of unity has not been breached, one might not expect to find love mentioned in a relationship involving merely spirit and pleasure, identically combined (Unity being a state of identification between opposites). But does love exist in Unity? Of course it does, depending on the particular society. But I have elsewhere indicated that in many Eastern societies, love is optional, men, if not women, frequently indulging in sensational sex in what appears to be an innocent manner.

In the West however, where we are, in general, more conscious and more individuated—that is, outside Buddhist monasteries—not least due to our enforced antagonism to Nature, sensational sex is a rarity. Such practitioners as there are belong to the 'creative classes' such as artists, musicians, dancers, and the like, who can perform decently though not necessarily with long-term commitment. The rest of the population don't usually perform decently, because most of them *attempt to regress to the original, sensational state of unity. It is the attempt to regress which debases half-individuated man.* The point is that, because the East has never breached the original Unity, it has never become individuated; there are, perhaps, no individuals in the East apart from Buddhist monks.

It is interesting to trace the line of evolution, or individuation, through history and by continents, or hemispheres. It is generally held that man first appeared in the continent of Africa—say, a million and a half years ago; while I would not dispute this, I do dispute, most strongly, the claim that man spread outwards from Africa and that every other race is indebted to Africans for its ancestry. This is yet another example of the half-baked thinking of science. Are Europeans descended from coal-black Africans, with their marked facial characteristics? Perhaps we were bleached by the snow? But I don't see any of my African friends turning white with cold. Perhaps our lips reached a reduced size by drinking out of 'Thwaites' beer bottles? Reams have been written about this supposed descent; it is taught authoritatively in our schools. Are scientists to be allowed to pontificate from their habitual basis of profound ignorance? Let them fire rockets into the air, at which they are good, but let them not profess to think; where did Sigmund Freud and Darwin get us?—shagging like emus and a dead God.

If *we* got white skins, how come the Chinese got yellow ones?—and slit eyes? Is there something special about the Chinese climate, the water they drink? Slit eyes, of course, could issue from water-borne diseases... I have yet to see a black man turn into a yellow one; maybe the snow turned *us* white, but I don't think Chinese piss turned *their* skins yellow. Think, lads.

Continuing our journey through evolution, I shall tell you something of further interest, and of direct relevance to the above passage. Consider, o'ye of lowly wit: why, but for reasons of consciousness, are Europeans white? That is to say, why are we in such close proximity to cold and ice?—in contrast to the steaming heat of unconscious, black Africa? Why the half-coloured skins of semi-conscious Asia?

From light, or consciousness, to dark, or unconsciousness, via semi-dark, or half-consciousness: does this not, at least, *suggest* something? As we all know, Africa has never evolved at all, living in primeval darkness, while most *individuals* in the world live in a state of mental enlightenment, in Europe or countries of European origin. Asia lives in a half-tone of semi-enlightenment. Do you see no pattern?

Any pair of opposites that is dissociated within itself—that is, one opposite dissociated from the other—automatically means dissociation within the psyche as a whole—leading at once to obscenity. The opposites may be separate, but if they lose contact, and become divorced, then they also become perverted. Perversion is but one thing: dissociation, and, consequently, exaggeration. There are very few socially-condemned perversions that aren't sanctified by love—including homosexuality—because, once within love, they become transformed and acceptable. Who is to say that any manifestation of love is wrong?

Returning to individuality, it is a fact, totally

unremarked by anyone, that the Eskimo people have no concept of the ego, or 'I'. The term 'I' does not exist in either the Eskimo language or psyche; the blinding implication is that *individuality itself* does not exist in this society, *which is therefore totally collective.* As in all collective societies, there is no difference between the psyche of one person and another (if indeed the word, 'psyche', is applicable) which is why, in many primitive groups, or races, it is possible to offer one's wife for the enjoyment of the casual visitor. Where there is no individuality, there is no jealousy—*for all are One,* primitive people living in a state of unconscious Unity.

However, to transfer this 'oneness' to civilized society is to invite disaster, *for it entails a regression to the former state of identification, or Unity* — an impossibility, attempted, nevertheless, by masturbation. Every time you attempt to have intercourse on a sensational basis, you are regressing to a condition which is no longer real in the psyche of civilized man.

Unity, as exemplified by Africa, is a condition of total, unconscious darkness, in which all is Oneness; there is no difference, or separation, between the opposites, and no difference between people. There is in fact no 'psyche', because, the psyche being mind, there is no difference between the conscious and unconscious functions: *there is no consciousness.* Black, or dark, skin indicates unconsciousness. The icy North breeds consciousness, and therefore the white skin of light. Yin and Yang present themselves here: the light of consciousness, the dark of unconsciousness. Africa has never evolved, because it was never its destiny to evolve; Europe and Asia evolved because it *was* their destiny. It is nevertheless Africa's fate to evolve in the future, at the hands of European consciousness—if Africans will let us. Colonialism was the best thing that ever happened to them. Mugabe was the product of their own, natural self—the dark, dangerous atavism, emanating from the 'dark' continent.

Darkness does include innocence; but innocence includes the potentiality for wickedness. And in the light of European example—sexual and militaristic—Africa was set ablaze, with lust and violence. Nothing is so wicked as Nature perverted, and now we see murder, pillage and gang-raping right across the continent. All according to the Image—an image already in the unconscious of the negro, but activated by contact with Europeans. This is the negative side of European civilization, but it works upon pre-existent susceptibility; no-one is more impressionable than the African.

The macho image extends from militarism to sexuality, where sex completely loses its identity—in the face of lust—and all semblance of reality. The poor women, as ever, are left holding the baby.

We see, therefore, both in Africa and in Asia, how

Nature, or natural man, can be perverted. In Asia it is common to see women 'bred to sex'—or bred for sexual purposes from birth; it is partly instinctive, being instilled by the erotically-demanding, social climate, and partly congenital after centuries of this lascivious indoctrination. How often have you seen the popeyed face of an Indian whore?—married or not?

India has never left unity. For all the consciousness of Buddhist monks, even they have never emerged from the womb of Nature, their brand of consciousness being but semi-conscious. To be fully conscious, one needs to be an individual—that is, to marry unconsciousness with consciousness—but as the Buddhist mind does not admit even the concept of individuality, and as, further, it is unaware of the existence of its own unconscious half, it cannot possibly individuate. Indeed it is entirely unconscious that it has either a conscious mind *or* an unconscious mind—which, by that fact, it hasn't. I just hope that there are some Buddhists not too blind to the Western discovery of the mind's dichotomy during the twentieth century. But then, dichotomy, or duality, is another thing Buddhists don't accept.

But if they don't accept the basic dichotomy of opposites—produced by consciousness—they have no chance of accepting consciousness, either. *There is, of course no dichotomy in unconsciousness, or Unity.*

It is the dilemma of Western man that he has to effect

a reconciliation between conscious and unconscious, which entails a return to the original Unity, or unconsciousness. But he cannot return without his conscious mind—recently discovered—behind him. It is the attempt to return without his newly-discovered, conscious nature, which is the problem; for, in eschewing his individuality, or consciousness, Western man becomes, or attempts to become, collective again: individuality cannot be reversed; there is nothing worse than the dissolute intelligentsia. The dropping of trousers for the first woman who comes along is directly contrary to the principle of the One And The Many. For, the One represents, in this case, the individual, the Many represent collectivity.

*   *   *

That is the problem; now for the cure.

The cure takes place again through the Sphere, but philosophically, with the Spiritual Body in mind. The Sphere might be said to *symbolize* the Spiritual Body. Learn to envisage, or imagine, the Sphere, both philosophically and intuitively, or consciously and unconsciously; in other words, metaphysically.

The Spiritual Body is a concept, embodying a fact, whereby the physical world, specifically sex, is made redundant. The physical world does not exist anyway, and the symbol of the Spiritual Body,—the Sphere—merely shows us this fact. We see, in the symbol, that the three dimensions of space and time, i.e. existence, are marked by the circles, or ellipses. *These are the representations of movement, or unconsciousness. In contrast, we see the representations of stasis, or consciousness,* which are the three dimensions of time and space marked by the straight lines. Movement is nature, or natural life; stasis is consciousness, or the subjugator of life. Consciousness kills movement *and* life, which is why man, the masculine principle, is known as the 'destroyer' of life, and why woman, the feminine principle, nurtures life. Light destroys dark, dark gives birth to light; *for consciousness was born of unconsciousness.*

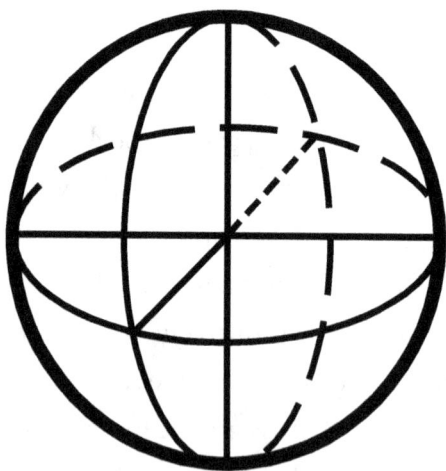

At the same time, consciousness creates: learn Paradox. Consciousness is what enables us to return to Unity, *or unconsciousness.* So we see that, ideally, conscious and unconscious would form a partnership: that partnership is provided by the Supra-Conscious—an amalgam of the two, which is the quintessential nature of the symbol. Light, or supreme consciousness shines forth—*in our minds*—effecting its healing as we think, and intuit. The succouring glow of consciousness makes itself more felt, more evident, with every faltering step we take—fusing together dissociated opposites and making us whole.

The nature of consciousness, in its position prior to amalgamation with its opposite, is to point the way to the cure, or to reconciliation with nature, or Unity. It cannot bring about the cure in itself; only in amalgamation with instinct, or unconsciousness, can it heal. *And then, of course, we have the ultimate Paradox. For, within the individual's mind resides the Supra-Conscious: conscious amalgamated with unconscious; that of the individual himself, and that of the cosmic symbol itself.*

* * *

A 'concept embodying a fact', of course, is a symbol. The concept is the mental image—or the visible part of the symbol—the fact is the meaning which the image represents: spirituality and physicality combined, or consciousness and unconsciousness.

The Spiritual Body combines the conscious and unconscious minds—not just in a symbol—but, nevertheless, what we are most concerned with *is the new age of symbolic reality*—first heralded at the end of the nineteenth century, by symbolist poets and artists, and brought, finally, by myself. Symbolic reality combines the spiritual, or mental, with the physical, or bodily, i.e. *the psychological*. The Conscious Psyche that I have promised (see 'Spiritual Body', Chapter on 'Sex', 1st issue 'Parsifal's Journal') is partly a body, but it consists of 'conscious meaning', or symbolism. A symbolic body is not a physical body: it spells the end of the physical world, and, along with it the *physical basis* of sex.

Though the symbol abolishes the physical world, it does so on the basis that the physical world is blind to itself—to its greater reality as the existential arm of essence, or mind. Combined with mind, the physical world finds its salvation, *and automatically becomes the Spiritual Body*.

Warp and Woof is the nature of the Cosmos, intricately interweaving its many and associated parts, as we have seen. Paradox is the name of the game.

While the Spiritual Body is a psychological phenomenon, it also contains a genuine body—*physical* reality, as we have just illustrated. The body, however, despite its necessity, is the poor relation; nevertheless, it achieves its salvation by mere association with its superior half. The sexual quotient is central here—taking 'sex' to mean Love. The three Cosmic parameters are: The One And The Many—the greatest principle; Self-Realization—the chief purpose; Love—the greatest Force. The chief opposites are consciousness and unconsciousness—or logic and instinct. All these combine to form the Sphere. But the greatest of all is Love. Love is consciousness: the consciousness *of* good, the consciousness *to do* good, the consciousness *of all knowledge*—its final repository; for, through Love, we know all.

Love, then, is the king-pin—beyond which 'sex' pales. Love contains sex—Love *is* sex—but it rises infinitely above it.

* * *

In as far as the image of the Sphere 'appears in front of us', we already know that it is a projection of the inner mind. Nevertheless, it is there to be contemplated, *with or without a visual configuration*. Its meaning is always present. But as a phenomenon, it is both subjective and objective—in particular, as a *symbolic* phenomenon. In other words, it *unites* inner with outer.

I have many times, elsewhere, described the relationship of the inner and outer minds: the symbol has an objective reality *outside the body, but not outside the mind.* For both the inner and outer minds—or inner and outer objects—are related by their original identification in the state of Unity. Thus, in the state of dissociation, they are parted. The Sphere appears, when bidden, to reconcile them—being projected from the one to the other—from inner to outer, at the same time appearing between as the Third Element, uniting them as One.

*   *   *

Existence consists of the three dimensions of space and time, but the fourth dimension, which the Sphere as a whole represents, takes us right out of existence into the Mind or Cosmic Psyche. The three initial dimensions of existence, as shown in the illustration, become the fourth dimension *by accumulation*; the fourth *is not added* to them. *Imagine this, because it is fundamental to the intuitive understanding of the Sphere.* You cannot 'see' the fourth dimension otherwise. See the Sphere *as a whole*, "the whole being more than the sum of its parts".

The Sphere, perhaps, does not appear to man except through the use of imagination and intuition, *because it is a symbol, and symbols are hidden. What we see is the visible, or illustrated image, from which we intuit the meaning beyond.*

Look within to find reality.

*   *   *

What, therefore, we *project* is the image, what we *intuit* is the meaning, but both internal and external reality are necessary.

The Spiritual Body is in fact the body you have now, *transformed.* The physical world, or physical existence, is God's gift to man, but it must find its greater reality in Mind—or that which lies beyond. Physical pleasure likewise finds its reality in the mind—revealing the blessing of Love.

Primitive man, or he who lives in Unity, *knows only the love of the One—that is to say, collective love, within which there is no such thing as individuality. Man, as an individual, does not exist, and consequently, individual love does not exist.* In the civilized state of disunity—or dissociation of opposites—we at least have individuality; but we do *not* have love. We must search for love, and adapt it, out of its unity, to the requirements of the individual. *If we find love in this condition, we will be reconciled with it in conscious Union—or re-union— reconciled with Individual, or Conscious, Love.*

A NOTE ON THE PSYCHO-PHYSIOLOGY OF SEX

In sexuality as in everything else, the elements of mind and body cannot be dissociated, though they can be separated.

To take the most obvious extreme: a sensation in the genitals. Such a sensation never takes place solely on a physical basis: we all know that; even a genitally-based sensation is largely psychological *in meaning*; if we don't know that, we ought to.

Starting from the Law of Opposites, the two most extreme opposites in the human body are the brain and the genitals; *but each commands the other*. The penis draws down the brain, the brain *informs* the penis. Without the relationship between mind and body, the body is mere trash, or discarded flesh, and the mind is a vacuous spirit. Hence flesh and spirit, the eternal contraries—the dark side to be explored by the light, or the unconscious to be explored by the conscious.

Taking the body as the unconscious, and the mind as the conscious, what do we actually explore? As we know, the unconscious is represented by the Whore, the conscious is represented by the Mother, or 'all things good'. For the mother to find her substance in life, she must explore the Whore—*and become the Whore*, since we are talking about the same woman, or Third

Element—that which rises between, and combines, the opposites, in a far greater whole ("the whole is more than the sum of its parts").

The Whore *is explored by* the conscious—in the passive state. *The Whore is done to. The body, therefore, receives the mind*, in most, if not all, of their relationship.

The genitals, then, receive information from the seat of the mind, the brain, though what is acting is the mind. The mind is in fact the only reality, the body being set up for no other reason than the implementation of, and enjoyment of, the mind. God is consciousness, or mind, and the Cosmos consists *solely* of mind, information proceeding from the outer reaches of the cosmic consciousness and reaching into the realm of physical existence, or the body, which, apart from the giving of pleasure, is a total illusion.

But, even then, the larger pleasure comes from the mind, though the most intensely-felt, *physical* pleasure lies, undoubtedly, in the genitals.

As to the actual *meaning* of pleasure, that comes entirely from the psychological aspect (that is, the mind).

(All these things are obvious, if you do but think about them.)

Proceeding from the general, now, to the particular, what was Casanova doing—as we all saw—in raking that adorable young woman into a heaven of delighted wickedness? Quite apart from presenting her, in her Naked Reality, before her Maker—for which she worshipped her dexterous lover—he was raking that delectable little clitoris into a tumult of pleasure. Mind to body, body to mind. Again, the genitals were one focus—minor, but vital—while the mind delivered its own goods: pleasure as contrasted with passion—pleasure felt purely physically, passion informing Casanova's love and his intense knowledge of Woman. In fact, in that scene we saw neither love nor mind, and were deliberately required to think that both were absent. For that, I hold the producer entirely responsible, and if this particular example of salaciousness is not to pervert every man, woman and adolescent in the country, it must be remembered that Casanova was nothing if not love—and not just a stallion. Lust being another name for passion, it finds its seat in the genitals and its inception in the heart—another centre of the mind. Centres of the brain control centres, or aspects, of the body; the clitoris, for instance, finds its controlling centre in the brain, while, at the same time, being under the surveillance of patterns, or ideas, in the psyche, or mind. The idea, transmitted to the clitoris, that it should feel a pleasurable sensation, is accompanied by the further suggestion that the feeling of pleasure should entail a psychological feeling of naughtiness (all this is obvious).

The thought emanating from the brain, or psyche, *resides in the clitoris, while the image of the clitoris resides in both the brain and psyche.* An image is partly physical and partly mental—anything visible necessarily being material. The mental element is the thought, or idea, while the physical element is the image sustaining that thought. The mental and physical elements together add up to the psychological whole, *the psyche itself being the combination of body and mentality.* This needs to be taken on board, because it is the answer to the 'mind-body problem' so dear to psychological science. The body contains the mind, the mind contains the body—a simple, though apparently elusive, fact which has served to bedevil contributors to the *Journal of Consciousness Studies* for at least a decade. The trouble ensues from the even more obvious fact *that physical existence is deemed to be all,* thus disguising mind from the consciousness of all scientists, who, though they may espouse the *idea* of mind, unconsciously dismiss it in favour of the solid and impenetrable appearance of bodily 'reality'. The operative word, here, is 'unconsciously', for even the impenetrable brain of a scientist would consciously accept that mind was paramount, even if it did not usurp the body. *Physical 'reality' is an absolute illusion, being merely the reflection of the mind behind it and containing it.* As the Archbishop of Canterbury never tires of telling us, the universe, and the earth contained in it, is a reflection of God's mind. Aristotle said so, as well—so *there*.

As this is a philosophical problem, rather than a scientific, or physical one, surely credence should be paid to the word of the greatest philosophical brains; and if Aristotle did not believe in God, that reduces his credibility amongst philosophers, since atheism issues from a fundamental and egotistical immaturity—not to say, neurosis. Atheistic intellectualism does not hold water, either, since it proceeds, not from an intellectual basis, but from pure assertion, guided by the assumption that man is as good as God—which issues, in turn, from science's self-proclaimed 'mastery of the physical world', beyond which it cannot see, being blinded by the illusion of the physical world itself.

* * *

Parts of the body are meaningless in themselves; in order not to become fixated on the tits, or the bum—or anything else—you have to move on—drawn up the body to the face: the magnetic-centre. If the parts are valued for themselves, they automatically become dissociated and exaggerated—the source of all perversion. Each element, or part, contains the whole body, the whole body contains each element, or part.

What you make love to, in fact, is her face—those all-signalling eyes. But those signalling eyes are the window of the soul—and when *they* aren't signalling, you may be sure the parts of the body have taken on the job—moving from one to the other, but always dictated by the soul, or mind. When you open your legs—as wide as a tart's, flagrant in display—I would do anything for you. Indeed, my little Tart, I would eat you like an ice-cream—but only within love. Love not and be damned; *for both elements and whole are lost.* The tongue is only employed in the loving warmth of devotion to duty (sighs of fervour ensuing). My most probable reaction, however, is to stop her gap with my masculine accoutrements.

The element of motion is pre-eminent here, it being essential to keep moving from part to part, as is known by every tart worth her salt, from strip-tease joints onwards—otherwise, the eager punter becomes bored, assuming he isn't a pervert. But the real reason is not boredom but fixation; this little lady is talking to you: converse with her. By signalling with her body, if not her eyes, she is saying, for instance, "don't you admire my thighs, my swaying breasts, my voluptuous, and provocative, buttocks? Then, come on—give a girl what she is asking for," And what churl could fail to answer that,

You may object that we already know this; but I would say to you that, though you may *know* it, you aren't *conscious* of it. How many times have you spoken about it—called a tit a tit, a cunt a cunt—especially your wife's tits or cunt?—even more especially, in the heat of love? In the sanctity of the bedroom? How many times have you discussed, and employed, illicit sex—the sex of the brothel? *Have you ever become a whore?* For it isn't just a name—it's an experience. You have to adopt the whore's character, her nature. That takes conscious debate— conscious consideration—an *awareness* of what it means to be a whore. *For unless you are aware beforehand, you may adopt the wrong, inadvisable, traits. This is the purpose of debate. But, more, without consciousness, neither you, nor the Whore, nor love, exist.*

And without existence, of course, there is no motion, apart from anything else. For, motion, or relationship, is what keeps sex going: arse to head, eyes to cock, hairs to bosom. If you don't like these allusions—specific as they are—you don't know explicit sex, explicit pleasure, or, particularly, explicit love. All of which adds up, again, to personal non-existence. I define 'non-existence' as anything belonging to the realms of unconsciousness, or collectivity; only individuals think—individuality being the negation of collectivity—by which assessment I mean that anyone who thinks, or is conscious, thereby exists; *collectivity, or unconsciousness is, literally, non-existence. In the absence of individuality, you, personally, do not exist* (In point of fact, existence doesn't exist, either—so pinch yourself).

The quintessence of existence, however, *is perhaps relationship, or the movement from one opposite or area, to another.* Without movement there is no relationship, only a pathological existence, with one opposite being cut off from another. Hence, there is no Third Element, and, consequently, no Whole, i.e. man or woman—or the lover.

Relationships necessitate symbolism; that is to say, a connecting link between the inner and outer minds, or between the inner object and the outer object. The inner object is an image of the outer object, or a memory of the outer object after subject and object parted. We have, then, the subjective, or inner, mind, and the objective, or outer, mind. It is not immediately obvious that there should be an outer mind; I would refer you to the original state of unity in the psyche, which was a state of total unconsciousness. One day in the course of evolution, consciousness came along, and, with it, the cataclysmic schism between the conscious and unconscious minds, one of which—consciousness—became the subjective, or inner, mind, the other of which—unconsciousness—became the objective, or outer, mind. The subjective, or personal mind looks outward, or downward, upon the objective or collective mind. I have proved elsewhere that external objects, as such, are artefacts of mind, not physical facts. Therefore, we are able to see that, whereas there was originally one mind, there are now *two*, separated by a schism.

It is the purpose of a symbol to connect the inner mind with the outer mind, or object. The symbol itself is an *invisible meaning*; it communicates itself by a *visible image*. In the unconscious state of unity, when mind was identified with body (or inner with outer) there was no schism between the two and hence no need for a symbol to connect them. In the unconscious mind of the primitive savage—the denizen of unity—there was no need for a symbol between subject and object; a *signal* there certainly was—otherwise the genitals would never have been alerted—but a symbolic image connecting the subject, or mind, with the genitals, or object, would have been redundant. A mental stimulus would have arisen from the presence of his partner, and been transmitted immediately to the genital region, but any intermediate stage would not have occurred. It was not necessary for any imagination to take place, as, between primitive man and woman, there is no barrier of consciousness, and therefore no need to invoke 'memories of time past'. Woman seduced man, and man was seduced— immediately—which is why, in so many primitive countries, women are kept in purdah: their men's parts are instantaneously aroused. Minds, no: they have no minds, only collective mentalities.

So we see why, in civilized man and woman, a symbolic image arises and is necessary. But one meaning of love, the reason why it is so important to civilized man, *is that it heals the schism between the inner and outer minds*, in combination with the symbolic image; for, *without* love, you cannot contact the girl's mind. Apart from anything else, you would not acquire the manners to approach her, and, like a boor, you would very likely strip her bra off before she was ready, or put your hand inside without being invited; but, worst of all, you would not have her interests at heart, and go at her like a bull at a gate, in a blind, masturbatory attack. Masturbation arises from the inability to effect contact between the two minds: both yours and hers, and also the inner and the outer.

For civilized woman represents the outer, or objective, world, whereas, in the savage world, there is no difference between inner and outer, and, consequently, man and woman are 'joined at the hip'.

Love has to be contacted in order to draw down information to the genitals, from the woman's initial consent—and yours—*and to establish the 'psychological meaning' (as above) between the two of you as well as within yourself.* The symbolic image conveys this meaning.

So, love, and mind your manners,—except when she wants you to be rude,

The image has to be thrust in your face, otherwise the 'vicar's daughter' won't acknowledge it. That is my job, and why I will be prosecuted time after time;—before I presented it to you, were you *conscious* of it? Sexual sport has to be rude—that is the essence of it—otherwise it can't be enjoyed. Men and Women are not satisfied by being 'nicely naughty'—which is what the spinsterhood believes. So, disport yourselves without restraint—and take my heartfelt blessing.

THE TRANSFORMING POWER OF LOVE
(LIBIDO)

The transforming-power of love has to be seen to be believed. In its wider context, this transforming-power belongs to the realm of libido, the background energy to the universe—in fact, the Cosmos. Libido is the energy of love, love is the ultimate expression of libido.

From whores to mothers, from hate to forgiveness, from cowardice to courage, love has the power to transform. But, in bed itself, we find perhaps its most intimate and sacred transformations. For, lust achieves beauty, a penis achieves nobility, violence becomes tenderness.

Always look at her eyes: they never lose their beauty, whether it's a loaded challenge, or a soft smile; it's all love, whether rude, passionate, or spiritual. And always it transcends the mere elemental qualities or parts.

The opposites are fused together whether by libido or by love, or by both together. Brain is fused to genitals, heart to whore—all unforgiving enemies, in their natural condition, which is why no-one can afford to ignore the factor of love and its reconciling properties. Reconciliation is, on the face of it, irrational; but, like most irrational things, it is full of reason. *The idea that two irreconcilable things could be reconciled is indeed irrational*, but the fact that it can be done is far from lacking in reasoned execution. If either opposite is taken out of context—that is, out of its relation to the other—then pathology ensues. That is rational. It is also rational to try and mend the rift. Where it may not be rational is in the 'being' of transformation itself—what 'being', at its essence, *is* rational? Is life rational? At the same time, it is my life's experience that not a single phenomenon is entirely, or even mainly, lacking in reasoned explanation. The 'irrational', in fact, is only that for which we have not yet found the reason. The only truly irrational thing is the state of madness—though even that has a rational cause and a rational cure.

To mend the rift, the humble human being can do a most positive thing: *he can put himself on the Cross.* That is what the Cross is for. *To fuse the opposites, or the two arms of the Cross, the martyr must endure. If each opposite is endured in equal measure, fusion will automatically take place, and relief will be obtained. This is the simplest, but most significant, fact of human existence.*

This, of course, is not directly the influence of love, though it is the influence of libido—the transforming power of such. But love most certainly can place us on the Cross, and it can equally certainly work the cure. Faced daily with a potential erotic dilemma, every one of us experiences the trauma of the Cross: penis torn from brain, heart torn from head, etc., and it is, indeed, love that saves us. If we allow it, the heart itself will direct us. The 'being' of love, of course, is only to be experienced, hardly explained.

The 'obscenities of love' are transformed *within* love. Flesh becomes a body *within mind*; love comes from a mind, an individual; love *entails* a mind, an individual, within which are transmuted all anarchies and atavisms—*in which coexist all contraries, separate yet united, in the greater whole of You and Me.*

CHAPTER III

The Secret of Desire

The secret of desire is peculiar to the Cross—that is, to the contemplation of the Cross. There have, in history, been one or two remarkable men who found an answer to desire, including C.G. Jung and the Buddha. I do not know what their solutions were, but mine is radically new—radically new but based on certain obvious facts. The first obvious fact is that of consciousness, and the power of consciousness to overcome all evil; for it is in the very contemplation of desire, and the evil done in its name, that we are enabled to free ourselves from what has all too often become its curse.

So hold to the Cross, ye good people, Stand steadfast between Yea and Nay—between Life and Death. Betwixt Life and Death—in the very Living-Death—we find the Middle Way; that is, the way to Eternal Life—our very tangible reward for the sacrifice of mortal life.

Standing mid-way between Yea and Nay, we survey desire—that is, spirit and flesh[2]—*and in the very ferment*

2. I include spirit within the concept of desire, because desire, properly speaking, is a 'spiritual' thing, having won—over its adversary, lust—and found a new innocence within the boundaries of love.

of this conscious process, we will subdue the power of the object—the sexual object. Reduce everything, I say, to consciousness, and desire will dissolve before your eyes. The twenty-first century Christian message is this very fact—a simple fact, but one which eludes us by its very obviousness. The act of consciousness, the act of thinking, is what displaces lust—for, what we are faced with, what makes it necessary to overcome desire, is its very perversion. Let those who are happy with desire, within the confines of love, pursue their blessed way; but we who are less fortunate can only find salvation by exorcising our evil—but then, what a glorious future awaits us, We have the possibility of individuality, of consciousness, of Eternal Life, "The Lord loves none so much as a repentant sinner." Only by dying do we become immortal.

Strung on the Cross, as you are, suffer your travail gladly; at the very point of lust, within its very fires, strive might and main to subject it to consciousness, to analysis; it can be done. Read my extensive philosophy on the subject, *and apply it*—right in the teeth of perversion. Reduce it to heavenly light, thus sublimating it. The cathartic image will assuredly arise—*between* the opposites, *between* spirit and flesh.

Will, also, that love should fill your heart, for not even consciousness *by itself* will effect the cure. *Will* love *into* the object, the naked body. And, above all, *paint* her, Worship your nude, with all the conscious knowledge that my work can give you.

*   *   *

I know all too well that there will be back-sliding—nothing is sweeter than lust: we *need* an orgasm—of whatever sort—so, every now and again, indulge—But always follow it up with a fervent embrace—a conscious embrace—of the beloved, whether the naked body or the image in mind. And remember: this is the very Battle For Life,

I am not saying that we should give up sex; I am saying that we must free ourselves from its compulsion. Assuredly, that is to die, but what of the riches to be gained? We are freeing ourselves of 'sex'—that is dying, dying to mortality, but in so doing we are partaking of Divine Love, as found in the Eternal Abode.

Unfortunately, Christ himself is not allowed either to live or to die, but only to endure endless torment; but *his* is *consciousness*. Gradually he sloughs off the guise of the flesh, raising it to spirit thus overcoming the power of evil. As he rises heavenwards, the dross falls away, revealing the mystical 'spiritual body', in which all opposites are reconciled—an emblem to inspire and comfort mankind for the next two thousand years.

*　　*　　*

Taking the measure of spirit and flesh—this is the surest way to consciousness; stand mid-way between the two and let them ebb and flow—for they are but phantoms of thought. *Seize them as they happen.*

If you do this as often as possible, you will build up an indispensable body of self-knowledge—but, more than that, you will learn to live in the Present—the Eternal or Perpetual, Present. This is perhaps the most practical way of engendering Eternal Life within yourself; but it has to be performed on an hourly, even momentary, basis.

*　　*　　*

The 'cathartic image', in its most vital form, is neither more nor less than Christ on the Cross—the Crucifix. This is the most potent symbol.

Individual will must be distinguished from the Collective Will. It is quite correct to say that, despite consciousness, the physical, or *unconscious* element is still compulsive; but the point is that we have to take consciousness *into* the unconscious, *thus dying to desire*, and, in the process, depriving desire of its power. But what we find instead is salvation through the *immortal* spiritual-body, or cathartic image.

THE SAVING GRACE OF BEAUTY

I write this as a sequel to 'The Secret of Desire'.

The 'cathartic image', in common with the spiritual-body, is essentially a thing of beauty. Beauty both inspires this image and is inspired by it—within the mind of man. Learn to love and learn to beautify, for they are the same thing: an attempt to sublimate desire or the object of desire. As the alchemists tried to do, we are in the process of 'turning dross into gold'.

In fact we may never succeed in escaping desire completely, but we can master it to a great extent, little by little. *Become conscious of it; subject it to scrutiny.* Hold it at bay in the very heat of the moment; thus living yet dying—at once. This is the Cross, shared alike by God and man.

Take your ugliness—your lust, for we all have it—and will yourself into a state of grace. For 'grace' is always there, waiting for us to call it forth; only by willing it can we summon it. And here we have the crux of the matter: the junction of collective will and individual will. The collective will may be said to be synonymous with desire; the individual will is that which subdues desire—through consciousness. We have to drag desire, or experience, out of the unconscious; and this is an arduous and lengthy process, taking, perhaps, many lifetimes.

Those of you who are artists have taken the first step; drawing the nude figure is the 'order of the day'. For all us artists recognize beauty. Dragging ourselves out of the mire we may emulate Christ, in his bid to create—to become—the spiritual-body, exemplified by the ubiquitous crucifix.

*   *   *

In the on-going attempt to master desire, even though we may never fully realize our goal, the 'living-death' is our salvation. For why, indeed, should we overcome desire?— In order to live and die at once—to know the heavenly and earthly in one, extended moment—that is, the Eternal Life, the Perpetual Present: something far more than the mere sacrifice of lust. In dying, we find life; in consciousness we redeem carnality, by the very resurrection of forgotten instinct.

*   *   *

You might ask, 'What is the difference between love and lust?'

In the Beginning, or the original state of Unity, love and lust were the same; in this, the twenty-first century, they are diametrically opposed—there could not be a wider difference. We are enjoined to re-integrate the former similarity—not the original identity, but what must become the present union, incorporating the divergence. We can achieve this by two means: by love and by thought; for, by thought we resurrect love, and through love we reconsecrate lust into innocent Desire.

Unfortunately, in the ages ensuing from Identification, desire has taken on the guise of lust, and in the attempt to assert his emotional self, modern man finds himself subject to the perversion which lust entails; we are obliged to distinguish between desire and its unnatural state. Desire and lust must again become *one*, hallowed by love, which rises *between* them.

Individuality was bred between the opposites, its own consciousness springing from the study of spirit and flesh, or love and lust—such individuality as there is in the world being confined to a small intelligentsia, which would necessarily contemplate Good—or love—and Evil—or lust. The edifice of civilisation *was constructed over time*, the state of Unity being essentially timeless, or stationary; that is to say natural man, while being 'aware' of time, was not actually conscious of it, living, as he did, in an *unconscious* Immediate Present. Natural man was not conscious of the difference between lust and desire—until civilisation forced it on him (Eastern man has still, for the most part, not broken the bonds of unity, Eastern civilisation arising from a harmonious relationship with nature).

Individual, or civilised, love requires time to develop, and modern man, handicapped as he is by gross emotional immaturity, must realise that 'relationships' can only develop over a prolonged period; *he would do well to remember that lust bears no relation to love.* Furthermore, except in rare instances, it is impossible for modern man to cultivate a sexual relationship without love: *he is obliged to proceed in, by, and for Love; there is no other way.* Sex *is* love.

*   *   *

The phenomena of love and time are intimately connected; love and evolution, or the passage of time, develops over a very long period—that is to say, conscious love and the consciousness of passing time. From their inception in original unity, both love and evolution travel through civilisation and *as a result* find themselves required to perform an about-face; having reached the watershed of civilisation (indeed, encountering it at every step) they have to *return* to Unity in thought, and, by thought, to retrieve the true spirit of love. Time having been extended by conscious love, is turned on its head and required to perform involution—again through consciousness. Every act of love is thus subjected to consciousness and traverses the whole of evolution backwards—to find itself.

From ignorance, or the horizontal plane of Unity, the vertical structure of evolution becomes erected; the whole edifice of the third dimension begins here.

*　*　*

Open up the nuptials, I say, and let consciousness penetrate the bounds of Unity. For there, behind primitive man, stands the One Person. Let it not be said that 'primitive' love is impersonal; lacking individuality it may be, but the personal element has always been present—invisible, or unconscious, albeit. And love is infinitely personal whether 'behind' or 'in front of' the lover—an about-face, indeed: the One Person becomes the individual person—an 'individual' person being evident to, or conscious to, his or her partner—in other words, *before* her. Thus, the whole world opens up…

LOVE AND TIME

The relationship of love and time is manifold, as my various writings on the subject bear witness. But perhaps the focal area is that including will; nowhere is will more vitally tested than in the battle to subject love—or desire—to conscious debate, and, through that, to the differentiation of time itself. Again we see the antimony of flesh and spirit, the study of which facilitates all knowledge—the study of flesh and spirit, that is, right in the teeth of lust—or innocent desire.

Take the moment of orgasm: how do we subject that to 'sublimation', or to time's very differentiation? The purpose of sublimation is to separate (differentiate) one moment from another—indeed to separate all moments from each other—thus extending the moment of orgasm to an *infinity* of moments. Truly this takes the very *greatest* effort of will.

Subjecting the orgasm to consciousness, then, we open up, not just time, but also the whole of Creation: time is, time was, time will be—if we let it. Consciousness of time is a variable; meaning that the *spatial extent* of time depends on one's viewpoint, whether conscious or otherwise. Both time and space—or their concept—vary according to one's awareness of perspective; internal in the case of the former, external in the case of the latter. We may separate the two to infinity, but they are also identical entirely according to consciousness.

The sense of time and space—one might almost say, the sense of perspective—is what orientates us in existence, ordering, as it does, our   experiences on the one hand, our thoughts on the other. Time and space can well be regarded as synonymous for spirit and flesh, *being in this respect, redolent of humanity itself*, i.e. thought, or mentality, in the first instance, sensation, or the body, in the second. We are not talking of 'spirit' in the moral sense—though that could equally well apply, for, love and desire are also invoked.

Contemplate, then, the act of love, from its beginnings in the land of Unity to modern times: does it not speak of evolution—i.e. the development of individuality—and all this time in one moment? Hold the orgasm; make that one moment last for ever, that every moment may, in turn, become the One, Eternal moment.

I am in fact recommending the deliberate frustration, or control, of orgasm—*in order to learn everything; to learn all, one must sacrifice all—temporarily.*

LOVE, CONSCIOUSNESS AND ENERGY

The sublimation of energy is a conscious act; it follows that the conservation of energy is also conscious, depending, as it does, on the process of sublimation to a large extent. Conservation is nowhere more essentially engaged than in love, or desire.

The 'whore' is the personification of energy (use your imagination) and in taming this beast we are both sublimating and conserving the natural forces. The purpose of this process is, in a word, the creation of civilisation; the horizontal plane of nature, or Unity, becomes the vertical plane of evolution, or consciousness itself.

The 'runaway whore', or raw energy, fills the vats of nuclear-reaction, whether physical or mental, and her explosive nature can be either catastrophic or harnessed to the greatest good. Thus we have, whether psychologically, physically or mentally, a demon in our midst, who must be mastered; such mastery being brought about by love itself, or art, or religion, or thought—even science,—but, in my system, by a combination of all these, consciousness being visited upon them both severally and together.

LOVE, CONSCIOUSNESS AND
THE CONSERVATION OF ENERGY

The figure of the Cross was made conscious, by Christ, as a two- dimensional image; I myself am introducing the three dimensional image:-

The three dimensional image represents the development, in the mind of man, of the potentiality of the known two-dimensional image. The first and second dimensions arose concurrently, as the first dimension simply does not exist by itself; but the second and third dimensions have also arisen concurrently, as all three dimensions depend on each other and lead into each other. Dimensions in themselves do not exist, and only appear to do so as realised constructions or images; in themselves, dimensions belong to the pre-existent, Archetypal Blueprint.

Dimension number one is 'pure energy'—the background to or primordial essence of, the universe, either just before or just after its creation (depending on the relative notion of time and timeless). By tracing a line from the earliest forms of life upwards, we can envisage the development of the three dimensions in animal (including human) consciousness. It is probably not possible to determine at what stages in animal-life consciousness itself developed; but, by using your imagination, you can see the creation of natural forms, from the beginning of time onwards, as fashioned by the cosmic consciousness or Archetypal Blueprint. In as far as forms were created by some 'agency' it is obvious that consciousness was employed in their creation, but only latterly did consciousness arise *within* them.

Without entering into a discussion of the origin of form, or forms, let me just say that consciousness was crucially involved here, and that, because the universe is a self-evolving epiphenomenon (an idea that science would probably not decry) consciousness progressed from the originating agency to—that is, into—the minds of individual creatures. In so far as nature—the handmaiden of the creating agency—herself possesses a mind,—and a mind need not indicate a personal incumbent—she, indeed, desires the creature, man, to harness consciousness to his own ends; to become, in fact, master of the universe.

We have of course, to harness not only consciousness, but also, through consciousness, its partner, energy. Energy has actually been harnessed unconsciously through Love—and, of course, through science, or technology. (Science, in itself, is not a conscious medium, as it lacks, in most of its practitioners, the element of true reflection, or thought, which only comes about as an amalgam of cosmology and applied knowledge.) Consciousness is indeed the main instrument in the taming of energy, chiefly by means of form, the very edifice of creation itself; invisible form—that is, potential, or unrealised form—belongs to the 'heavenly,' or pre-existent, realm of the Archetypal Blueprint, to which also belongs potential dimensionality—that being interchangeable with the concept of form. Form itself arises on the crest of consciousness and energy—that is, on a wave created by the *application* of consciousness *to* energy, which 'freezes' energy, effectively, and produces a visible line, or that which *defines* form.

By 'harnessing' energy I do of course mean 'sublimating' energy, and this requires the two instruments of Love and Consciousness, coupled with the 'cathartic image', which takes place, of course, through the further element of Imagination. As I have explained the process of sublimating—to some extent—elsewhere, I shall not digress at this point.

Unity, or the circle of energy, becomes, through time, or evolution, civilised or conserved energy, disposed within love—or individual love. Unity, or *collective* love, only exists in the Collective Mind; therefore, particular collective mentalities do not exist; nor does collective love, since it is not envisaged, or brought to consciousness. It may be *known*, but since when has *instinctive* knowledge breached the bounds of unconsciousness?

Conserved energy is the purpose of evolution, erecting the edifice of the Cross, vertically, on its horizontal base, or the dimension of *raw* energy. Consciousness rises upwards, unconsciousness remains 'flat' or unremarked. Conservation harnesses the *power* of energy, to creative purposes; raw energy is untapped, and therefore dissipated in the jungle of unity. (From this it can readily be understood why Africans in general, and other races, have more energy than the Whites, since they are closer to the earth, or the state of unity.)

Conscious love both creates, and is created by, individuality.

(Throughout this essay, 'form' should be regarded as synonymous with 'dimensionality').

A NOTE ON 'SUBLIMATION'

Sublimation being one of the more arcane subjects with which I deal, and playing a very prominent part in my general exposition, could be left largely to the reader's engagement with the body of the book; however, perhaps I should briefly annotate a few points here.

We have the single 'object'—say a stone, or a building; further, we have the 'objective' environment. Both serve as representatives of the 'outside world' but let us take the sexual object i.e. the body, as our example. The sexual object is particularly susceptible to sublimation because it holds such power over us humans, as can readily be seen. We are enslaved by, and decimated by, the power of this object, or indeed of any object; it exerts a tremendous influence on us, both physically and mentally. Therefore, it would be of great advantage to us if we were to get rid of it. Perhaps the only way to get rid of it is to 'sublimate' it—to make it vanish—to deprive it of all power; and the best way to do that is to *withdraw* its power into ourselves.—'Necromancy', you say; and what's wrong with that? Witchcraft can be very effective—it does work.

But witchcraft aside, the actual mechanism of sublimation is quite logical; in order to sublimate the sexual object, we have to master desire: to sever the object from the subject (ourselves), to withdraw *from* the object its power to attract us. If desire vanishes, so does the object—or at least, it becomes impotant. So how do we set about mastering desire?

Probably the most effective way to reduce desire is to become an *artist*. Anyone, in fact, can become an artist; painting, or drawing, is the one art anyone can learn, and was sent to us for the specific purpose of sublimating desire. 'Distance yourself from the object' is the divine injunction, and by drawing the naked body you do just that. Observe the contours of this lady's lovely figure: what are they saying to you?—"Love me, cherish these lovely parts." There are in fact many ways in which to implement the mastery of the art of drawing—that is, specifically, to master the object. Perhaps the most important is Love: *draw with love*; the human body was designed to inspire love—not lust—and through this divine medium you can, if you are diligent, acquire some of that divinity yourself. All the great artists had it, from Michelangelo downwards; they revelled in love; every day they became further removed from the object—by drawing. But not *simply* by drawing; they *consciously thought*; and through thought they drew down the divine, or heavenly, Promethean Fire—the source of all thought, formerly the property of the gods, now the instrument of humanity; thank these heroes for showing us the way.

Versed in love, or thought, then, we are enabled to describe, on canvas, *a divine image: the body, sublimated*. The transcribed image becomes 'divine' by the very act of transcription, or drawing—the transference of the contours of the body; *love* this body, *love* your drawing— love all bodies, all women. Soon you will rise above all earthly cares and concerns; no longer will you be ensnared by the wiles of the flesh.

Build up a philosophy, in partnership with art: *how* to love? *Why* love? *Why* do these specific contours conform to love, and not to lust? How are they formed? What is their purpose? How do they themselves describe the actual body? Draw them, and think.

Take them apart, one by one, and examine them; how do they fit together, how do they create the whole? Integrate them on the canvas, create the mysterious Third Element for yourself: "that which lies, or arises, between"—between the subject (yourself) and the, by now, powerless object.

Integration itself—the goal of civilisation in the wake of Nature's fall from Original Unity—appears on the psychological horizon, drawing together the dissociated strands of the Self, which was vitiated for millennia by the

Demon Object. Nevertheless, the Object remains, divested of its potency but not actually extinguished; we may *return* to the Object, but not, this time, as its slaves. Sex, or Love, is a gift—the gift—which may not be abandoned—once we have learnt to direct it.

All danger, then, being removed, all compulsion reversed, perfect freedom issues in our midst. Sublime you now are, sublime you ever will be; one foot on earth, one foot in heaven.

*   *   *

I desire the various parts of a woman's body; therefore I *don't* desire them. What is mine to will is mine to will not.

It is a question, though, of individual and collective wills. The average man is subject to the collective will; it is his task to wean himself away from the collective and onto the individual, where he can exert his own will.

First, one must become aware of the possibility of this: if one thinks it is impossible, it *will* be impossible. *One is enabled to exercise will if will is made conscious, so freeing it from its unconscious, or collective, boundaries.* By this relatively simple act, the problem is solved. It does, though, take time to build up the necessary *willpower*—which, nevertheless, depends largely on conscious persuasion.

Realise that you desire; realise that the collective will

is desiring *through you*—which makes desire itself irresistible. *Disassociate yourself from desire, which is a collective thing.*

Nevertheless, it is not possible to entirely disassociate ourselves from desire: we are human; we live. Therefore, the only measure is sublimation, as above. Hold to the Middle Way—the way of sublimation, where a body becomes the Spiritual body, and not subject to compulsive desires. Let emotion and passion rule you, through the Heart, not the genitals. Titillate yourself, if you like, at the sight of a woman's bum, or tits, but always refer this genital pleasure to the emotional centre, or Heart.

*   *   *

PREAMBLE TO:
'THE NAKED SAVAGE HOLDS THE SECRET'

We have had 'pleasure within love'; now how about exploring 'love within pleasure'?

The first thing to strike us is the situation of reverse images; i.e. 'pleasure within love' vis-à-vis 'love within pleasure'; in other words, exterior vis-à-vis interior, and interior vis-à-vis exterior—exactly the centripetal-centrifugal antimony. (The centripetal and centrifugal forces, fundamentally at work in the universe, have a great deal in common with Jung's concept of extroversion-introversion, or projection-introjection, though they take the original idea much further. Jung's bequest to us was the greatest intellectual, and scientific, idea in the history of thought).

The basic fact about our universe is that it is constructed, and conducted, on the basis of the centripetal-centrifugal principle; that is to say, the principle of expansion-contraction, which is derived from it. We have, on the one hand, man, representing the particular, and on the other hand, the universe itself, the universal; complementing this idea, we have that of the Sphere—or my concept of the universe as an 'expanding-contracting sphere'. Man, the tiny point at the 'centre' of the universe, in the position of the particular, expands far beyond himself to the outer reaches of the universe; the universe correspondingly contracts to the point of man, from the position of the universal. This perpetually mobile relationship illustrates that of the Whole and the Parts, which are related intimately and constantly in the same mode. The relationship of Whole and Parts, or Universal and Particular, pervades all aspects of life (including the very restricted area of physical existence) from psychology to the splitting of the atom, and is based, of course, on expansion-contraction. It is also a basic fact, about this relationship, that the universe and man are connected physically; that is, by a physical tie—something resembling an umbilical cord: Mother Nature giving birth to, and sustaining, her human brood (for in this case the umbilical cord is permanent). In this wise, also, is conducted the relation of man's soul to the Lord above; and, here, we are talking not only of Jung's conception of the soul, i.e. the 'anima' (or 'animus'), but also of the obvious connection of the 'immortal' soul to the heavenly regions. I do not think Jung was aware of the full implications of the term 'anima', for it possesses a double meaning: one, the obvious reference to the 'animating principle' within the human psyche, but, two, the corresponding reference to the 'animating principle' *within the human body*. Leaving aside the dispute over body and psyche, let us take up the point of the immortal soul contained within the body; in fact the two adumbrated conceptions coincide, but what I am concerned with is the connection of man's bodily soul *with the soul of his Maker*; for, constructed on this connection, is the whole relationship of man and God, furthermore depending on the principle of expansion-contraction. Even such apparently nebulous concepts as the soul of man and the soul of God have a physical component—without which neither of them could exist—and the physical connection between them, i.e. the umbilical cord, is manifested by expansion-contraction: man's soul expands towards God, God's soul contracts towards man. Could you have a more fundamental, and significant, relationship than that?— From which is reflected every dual phenomenon in the universe—that is, every phenomenon determined by a subjective-objective antinomy, or that of the centripetal and centrifugal.

I find it necessary at this point to explain the inner workings of centripetality-centrifugality. Normally it would be the case that contraction 'contracts from' something rather than 'contracts towards' something—a physical impossibility—but what we are faced with is the essential Paradox of all life. Without Paradox we could not understand our world, and certainly not the fundamental centripetal-centrifugal idea, *which is founded on a simultaneous reciprocation between the two opposites.* Furthermore, this is a *double* paradox: while centrepality is expanding, it is also contracting; while centrifugality is contracting, it is also expanding; while the former expands, it is drawn out, or contracted by, the latter, which, while it contracts, is expanded into by the former. The Whole, while contracting, contracts 'something' into itself; the Particular, while expanding, expands, or projects, 'something' into the Whole; the 'something' in the case of the Whole is the soul of the Particular, the 'something' in the case of the Particular is its own soul.

While the particular is contracting, it contracts the soul of the Whole into itself; while the Whole is expanding, it is expanding, or projecting, itself into the Particular. All this is an essentially mutual and enhancing reciprocity.

If you doubt anything I have said, I can only inform you that you should do as I did, and pare down everything in the universe—everything from church sermons to tea-cakes—until you are left with nothing but the bare and naked essentials—the rock-bottom reality of God and man, an atom vis-à-vis an aspidistra.

You cannot see any of this, because in you the unity has not been broken. What you do, or see, is performed on the lid of unity without actually breaking it open. You may do, but you see not; Pandora's Box remains unexplored.

You may, if you are lucky, see pleasure within love, *but because you are not awake, you do not see love within pleasure.* The two are in fact mutually reflecting, as are all opposites, particularly God and man, but because, in you the opposites are identified—that is, in a state of indistinguishable unity—you fail to observe them, thereby relinquishing all possibility of understanding them. Their relationship must be understood, because otherwise there is no hope of the furtherance of evolution. *Evolution depends on you. Therefore, suffer, and thereby awake.*

The mutual reflection, or reversed image, of centripetality and centrifugality means that we have, once again, a double paradox, in that, centripetality, *casting outwards from within*, faces its complementary, centrifugality, *which draws inwards from without*. Two sides of the same coin, quintessentially represented by 'pleasure within love', and 'love within pleasure', the genie, within each, conjuring the other out—true soul-mates: indeed, Lovers. So flourish all Lovers everywhere.

CHAPTER IV

The Naked Savage
Holds the Secret

In the Words of Christ, or Parsifal, Himself

Pleasure must come from the heart.
Pleasure must be *given*.

* * *

For the next millennium, I, Parsifal, bring the following revelation:-

It is my intention to bring Venus, the representative of the female sex, for the first time to womanhood, she never before having known explicit, or real, pleasure—pleasure for the sake of pleasure; not *drowned* in love, but *guided by*, and *given by*, love. I, Parsifal, bring the boon of unadulterated physical pleasure to the civilized world for the first time; this precious gift from the Lord himself, to be cherished and respected.

But before this can come about, *the opposites have to be separated*; otherwise, neither pleasure nor spirit will become explicit, the explicitness of spirit, also, being desired, and following as a natural consequence from the isolation, or separating-out, of its complementary, pleasure. Man and woman, in this contemporary stage of evolution, remain unawakened; for them to achieve the knowledge of explicit sex, consciousness has to be introduced.

At present, Unity holds sway, Unity has not been broken; your life until now has been totally unconscious; that is why I have come—in order to implant the mind-set required for evolution's next purpose. The unconscious psyche, or collective unconscious, must be aroused to its own reality. In Unity, spirit and pleasure are indistinguishable; Venus *knows* pleasure, she *knows* the difference—she gives it to her lover every night—but she does not *see* it. She experiences it as Absolute Love, in which she is totally unaware. On becoming a Woman, therefore, Venus will for the first time know herself.

For, this situation, the independence of opposites from each other, has in fact always existed. Despite the state of Unity, i.e. unconsciousness, our little lady has actually known it, waiting only to be awoken to it. And so the Prophet has come to her for precisely that purpose. The opposites, apart in consciousness, have awaited the actual revelations of consciousness ever since the Prophet was prophesied— *right at the beginning of creation.* Foreordained, and previously existing, the separation of the eternal contraries has been awaiting the delivery of explicit discovery, within the minds of men and women, ever since the dawn of Conscious Knowledge was first forecast. This is what the world has been waiting for ever since its conception—this, the fulfilment of evolution's purpose, as promised by our Messiah, and accomplished by his death through his crucifixion.

Unity and the eventual state of re-Union co-exist in the timeless, yet are separated in time by the Schism of all opposites, so presenting us with the Eternal Present; Unity and Union, or consciousness and unconsciousness, themselves combine in the further result of the Supra-Conscious; both these results are what evolution is aimed at.

All this ensues from the presence of the Naked Savage, or the natural whore, at the centre of the unconscious. The natural whore is a paradoxical figure, being potentially both good and evil; innocence, or nature, is the state of good and evil combined in unrecognized form, the actual *knowledge* of good and evil being a conscious development, conferring recognition. Between the unrecognized condition and the condition of recognition, in other words between consciousness and unconsciousness, lies the Subconscious, where the relations of our whore's paradoxical nature are conducted. The Subconscious itself is also a particularly paradoxical area, through which all conscious-unconscious relationships pass, being in fact partly conscious and partly unconscious.

The paradoxical condition of the whore lies in the contrast between good and evil, which produces, through the relations of conscious and unconscious, what is actually a *multiple* paradox. We have, on the one hand, the *conscious* good and evil of the whore, and, on the other hand, her *unconscious* good and evil. That of which we are unconscious is natural and innocent, in other words, both good and evil; that of which we are conscious is *either* good or evil, thus losing its innocence. So the natural whore, according to whether we are conscious or unconscious of her, is *either* good and evil, or *both* good and evil. The state of Nature, or naturalness, depends entirely on the standpoint of the conscious or unconscious attitudes; *in itself, it does not exist, being a mere concept. The physical world thus vanishes, in a puff of mental smoke. This, ultimately, is what the whore brings to us; the study of sex, or love, reveals all.*

The exact proportion of conscious to unconscious, within the Subconscious, is impossible to determine, since it is a highly mobile, and paradoxical, area. Essentially it is neither conscious nor unconscious, but a buffer state, constantly adjusting its borders. Passing through the Subconscious, the whore metamorphoses from good to evil and back again, *according to our consciousness, or unconsciousness, of her*, initially proceeding from the state of innocence to the civilized state—again a paradoxical situation, since a civilized whore is presumed to be innocent while a natural whore is susceptible of the most distinct evil. Both the civilized whore and the natural whore are capable either of good or of evil.

The Naked Savage, representing, basically, instinct in general, is focused on the whore, and as such is subject to the same transformations. *But both her good and evil propensities are potential, not being realized until she comes into contact with civilization.* Civilization, being consciousness, works in direct opposition to instinct, or unconsciousness; civilization in fact suppresses instinct, so producing the most unnatural, and perverted, whore,—a creature, sworn to the destruction of her oppressor, who rampantly overtakes the civilized world. Civilization brings destruction on itself—even in Asia, where culture is largely based on friendly relations with Nature. The Asiatic consciousness has sprung from, and maintains contact with, its natural source—which, despite its obvious advantages has, nevertheless, prevented the East in general from breaking out of Unity; the Asiatic mind has never assaulted its unconscious. Brutal though it may be, the Western attitude to instinct has in fact enabled it to develop its own peculiar consciousness, and even a potential ability to achieve re-integration with its origins. Never having developed an awareness of its own Unity, Asia remains unconscious of the potential schism within it, even being unaware of a possible dichotomy between the conscious and unconscious minds; indeed the awareness that there is such a thing as the unconscious—and by implication, the conscious—probably has never occurred to the Eastern mentality. In the twentieth century, however, such a dichotomy as was discovered in the West, probably penetrated to the East.

*   *   *

Love Is All

Love is all,
Love was all,
Love suffuses all.
We make love for love, by love,
In love, through love.
Love knows all,
Love sees all,
Love is all.
Love is within it
And love surrounds it.

Moaning, and gasping with pleasure, at the extremity of her womanly endurance, she thrusts herself against me, meeting me strongly in my own movements, in the throes of purely physical ecstasy. For all my love, I do not wish her to be conscious of it, but simply to enjoy herself utterly just as every other adorable little whore in history, knowing only my irresistible masculinity and her own yielding femininity.

When she can stand it no longer, both she and I release ourselves into the final crescendo of eternal, and carnal, Knowledge. Just before she experiences her inevitable Annihilation, she cries, "Fuck me to death," And I do, with all the incredible love and adoring assiduity that only the Supreme Lover is capable of. There is no love without love.

Know that thou art being fucked. But never doubt, deep down, that it is coming from me—never doubt my loving adoration for you in your extreme and sublime moments.

When she recovers consciousness, she is aware that she has been given love, not just physical satisfaction, and she relaxes in my arms in the fervently grateful knowledge of it. While being given such pleasure, she knew, however unconsciously, that she had given herself to my care for the purpose, after all, of love, and nothing but love. But my wanton little sweetheart must be made aware that she is unmistakably receiving pleasure. For despite its unreality, the need for pleasure is real—to be enjoyed in and for itself.

In being annihilated, she is transported into a world where life not only ends, in such fire, but also begins again. The whole of the extended life and death cycle is experienced in one united moment.

Become conscious of it.

*   *   *

Far from the frenetic dissolution into nothingness sought by the Slut, where everything is destroyed—Including Creation itself—She and I are brought together in the ultimate knowledge of each other: a union not just of ourselves, but of ourselves and God also, in the very experience of his most reverenced gift.

Pleasure, having been so vital, dies in the face of its far greater rival.

*   *   *

But the most wonderful thing of all is that the girl she always has been will remain, alongside the woman. The exquisitely feminine, loving young girl will be transformed, alongside the Mother, into a passionate and needy Whore, abandoned to the loving attentiveness of her master. Mother and mistress will exist side by side.

Absolute love remains,
Adoration is realized;
And all because pleasure was *given*

*　　*　　*

THE PSYCHOLOGY OF THE WHORE

The twin sisters, the good whore and the bad whore, are actually identical, being present in every woman. It is woman's task, beginning in this, the twenty-first century, first to separate her two identities, and then to tame, or civilize, the errant sister. The errant sister, when civilized, will become the good sister. In the state of Nature, the whore, though uncivilized, can certainly be good, or innocent, but her potentiality for evil, *only awoken, paradoxically, through civilization's influence*, is prodigious.

This paradoxical exchange necessarily takes place through the Subconscious, the very home of paradox, being the crossroads between conscious and unconscious, or civilization and nature. The Subconscious is, indeed, the focal area of the good and evil antinomy. The transactions between good and evil, constantly emerging into consciousness, then re-submerging into unconsciousness, *are essentially in a state of flux in order to facilitate conscious debate, for it is only within this mobile paradox, this ever-shifting scene, that the secret of good and evil, even that of life itself can be found.*

The contamination of the natural whore, by contact with civilized society, means that Nature herself faces destruction, Nature herself, of course, being innocence and also, therefore, all that is right. We come, here, upon a further paradox in that, innocence, while consisting of both good and evil, *also consists of neither.* This paradox arises from the conscious attitude within the Subconscious, which alternates with the unconscious attitude, also within the Subconscious, to the effect that the contradictory situation, which is also apparently unresolvable, becomes resolved in the acceptance, again, of a *multiple* paradox; accepting both the fact that good and evil are present, and the fact that neither of them is present—and this simultaneously—we are enabled to realize that all facts, by implication, are merely concepts within an alternating conscious attitude; in other words, all facts are elements of mind. The physical world, therefore, being the *ultimate* fact, is thus shown to be a vast illusion, having reality only within itself, conferred on itself by itself.

Good and evil, then, being alternating mental concepts, the one becoming the other, the other becoming the one, it becomes obvious that the whore cannot reliably be judged to be either good or bad; a state of neutrality, you might say. How, then, does she come to be evil, or alternatively, good? It is, of course, a matter of moral standpoint—you might say, a matter of opinion. But if we discuss the concept of evil as a matter of opinion, we open the floodgates to whoredom. There undoubtedly is such a thing as whoredom, whether as a concept or a matter of opinion, *or as physical fact.* Given that physical facts are an illusion, what conclusion can we come to? Is whoredom after all an illusion?

Within the physical world, as we have seen, *reality does exist, relative to itself.* In this light, whoredom can be seen, after all, as a physical fact with some reality. As we do, after all, live in the physical world, we have to abide by physical facts *and also by physically-driven laws.* Even our moral laws have a physical basis, being derived from a physical sense of conscience, or shame, which penetrates to the mentality in the form of the soul, which is the seat of self-respect. As science knows, all phenomena without exception have at least a component of physicality, this being true even of the soul; thus, even self-respect is partly physical. We begin to see a certain connection between the world of ideas, or concepts, and the physical world, each obviously containing an element of the other. We may substitute consciousness for concept, and unconsciousness for the physical world, for if the physical world were conscious, it would know itself to be an illusion, meaning that whatever reality it has is entirely unconscious, and residing within the sleeping mentality of man. Concept, or thought, is by definition conscious, nevertheless containing unconsciousness, while physicality contains an element of consciousness, *these two paradoxes only being possible within the Subconscious, which mediates between the conscious and unconscious modes.* Consciousness constantly emerging from the dark recesses of its opposite, which equally constantly reclaims it, we have before us the essence of the Subconscious, and it is there we must look for the secret of the Naked Savage, the whore, and the secret of life itself.

The crucial fact about the Naked Savage, or the natural whore who represents her, *is that neither of them is able to see,* being so essentially contained within the unconscious that no thought, or consciousness, penetrates; the unconscious knows, but it does not see. This being so, the Naked Savage is totally unconscious, and from this follows the basis of all human psychology, for while man, or woman, is fundamentally unconscious, the whole purpose of our being on earth is to raise this very unconsciousness to a conscious level, to expose it to the light of day, thereby enabling man to see himself, where, before, he was able only to *know* himself. The significance of this requirement for the further development of evolution is incalculable; from being a totally physical, or unconscious being, man is now on the threshold of becoming a psychological being. He is beginning to think for himself, whereas, previously, the common man has relied on the philosopher to do his thinking for him, which is, or was, the philosopher's job. The philosopher should now be redundant, being displaced by the rising commonality of humanity.

Buttocks and Pork

Pleasure deals in the flesh,
But I don't.
I deal in passion,
Which skirts on the flesh, but does
Not include it.
Buttocks look their very worst when
Subjected to scrutiny
Thus being deprived of their connection to the passion-
filled body
Denuding them of their properly made attributes,
And reducing them to flabby pork.

*   *   *

The unknown mystery of love is yet to be known.
Wills it?
Wills it not?
Listeth it?
Listeth it not?

*   *   *

Life is an adventure between whole and parts;
From the painting of a picture to the thrall of
lovemaking,
We experience the workings of universal and particular,
Taking in the One—
Or the mysterious One Woman—
To the Many,
Or the equally mysterious Whores;
For, of Whores there are many indeed,
But of Mothers, only One.

For the Whore to be saved
She would have to become One;
And likewise do we see
The whole history of man-and-woman kind.

*   *   *

We are being asked to conjoin illusion and reality,
To realize that pleasure and the whole venal entourage
Are outrageous illusion
—If taken on their own—
And that, whatever purpose they do serve,
Is not the purpose of Love,
Which is the only reality,
Coming first, last, and foremost

*　　*　　*

The body is the temple to the soul,
Not the incarcerator of fleshly folds.

*　　*　　*

The common man is for the first time within reach of individuality, in other words, of a *unique consciousness*, which secures his independence and freedom. *There is no such thing as political independence or political freedom*; no country is, or can be, independent of any other country, and the only freedom man will ever have is in the ability to think. The Declaration of Independence was a falsely conceived and disastrous imposition on the innocence of an unsuspecting world, being directly responsible for practically all wars and revolutions since that date. Man has absolutely no right, especially not a divine right, to any independence, or political freedom, whatever. Man has, in fact, no right even to a right. This impertinent assumption is based on the belief that man was put on earth to serve his own purposes, that he is somehow paramount in God's affections. While God may love his world, his own creatures, that creation is designed for His own purpose, which is, to reflect the glory and being of the Lord himself. *Man was created to serve God.* The only freedom he may have is attained through thinking, and designed solely for the further glorification of his Creator. God may be an egotist, but that is his prerogative. Up there in heaven, he has nothing else to do but contemplate himself, through man. That is his right, and the poor buggar hasn't got much else. (The only woman he has ever loved awaits him on earth, unknown to herself).

The fundamental fact that God's only comfort is the contemplation of his own self, is the reason for his creation of the world, and man is only in it for that end. The further fact that God so loves his world that he periodically comes to save it, being crucified for his trouble, should alert us to our iniquity in assuming our own importance; beyond God's love for us, we have no importance. But because man's own self-love, or ego, is so great and all-pervading, he actually assumes himself to be the equal of his Father. No son can be the equal of his father, because he simply isn't conscious enough, *but man is so egotistical that he will not allow even God to be his superior*. Thus the atheistic and scientific belief that man is paramount, and that God himself, as a consequence, is dead.

But God is very much alive—so much so that, witnessing man's iniquity he travels to earth, not so much to condemn him as to save him; and man, perceiving him—knowing full well who he is—denies his very existence, supplanting him with his own egotistical conceit, and, hating him so much for his intolerable superiority, he finally, and inexorably, puts him to death, hoping that he will never rise again, so proving that he is in fact so superior that he triumphs over death. In denying, furthermore, that there is life after death, man is attempting to prove, by this very belief, that God indeed doesn't exist, and that man himself, therefore, can bestride the earth, its master. And so all atheistical and arrogant belief is intended to destroy the very essence of life itself: the Eternal Return of all living phenomena.

Christ is on earth today to present once more the Truth: that God loves his creation, despite his creature's determination to destroy it—and, in the process, himself—to such an intensity that He has subjected Himself to unimaginable agony in order to ensure the survival of consciousness over unconsciousness. For, only in this event, will the future of the world, and man within it, be secure from the destructive powers of unconscious instinct, *in which resides all ego, lust, self-deception, and non-thinking.*

In saying God put man on earth for his—God's—own purposes, I do not mean that man is without a purpose of his own—God-given. It is man's duty, man's joy, to reflect the face of God; but, given this task, it is also man's obligation to obey the ways and laws of God.

As a phenomenon in the phenomenal world, man is a phenomenon in himself, as well as being a projection of the Lord; and as a *phenomenon in himself*, the human being has *one right*: to exercise his self-hood through thinking. Selfhood is endowed by man's phenomonality-in-himself, to be explored and enjoyed in, and for, itself. The wider issues of man's connection to the Lord, i.e. *beyond* himself—*or beyond the phenomenal world*—have still to be acknowledged and addressed, and the sole connecting-link between the two worlds is that of Thought—whether inward, or outward, looking.

*   *   *

If the opposites were severed, or divorced—as opposed to merely separated—a pathological situation would ensue: the whore would go one way, taking her knickers off for all and sundry, and the mother would go the other way, inviting the vicar round to put a damper on her husband's ardour; there would be absolutely no connection between.

The whore cannot be seen without the mother, for she is at once her restraining influence and the element of giving, the whore herself being simply the woman who receives, or experiences, pleasure. The bad whore is one from whom all connection with the mother has been withdrawn, thus being left without the capacity to give. It may be the mother who actually gives, but because, under natural conditions, the opposites are only separated, and not divorced, there is still a relationship between the two women. Although it is the lover's intention that his mistress should not be conscious of anything but pleasure, she very obviously remains aware, unconsciously, of the fact that she is being loved, and of who loves her. *She is in fact abandoned to love, not pleasure,—love suffusing, surrounding and superseding;* experience, or unconsciousness, does not lose its relation with consciousness, to which it returns at the moment of climax. Conscious love, the goal of the separation of opposites, is achieved when experience and consciousness are finally united in the fire of our Passion.

Through alternating consciousness and unconsciousness, whore and master conduct their love-making; for it is love. Although my little wanton is immersed in pleasure, both of us surface periodically to take conscious stock, our unconscious knowledge receiving conscious recognition in the presence of our mutual love. And then we return again to our abandonment to pleasure; always giving, always receiving. Spirit and earth never came so close together, unknown to themselves in the one instance, yet trumpeted abroad on emergence into the other, continuing constantly in the gradual accumulation of conscious-experience, their desired end.

*   *   *

PORTRAIT OF A SEXUAL ENCOUNTER

This strumpet, who lures every man to her ever-waiting cunt, was proceeding down Oxford Street in her usual fashion, salaciously dressed—that is to say, with every part of her body under a minimum of disguise—and swinging her hips in a way that protruded her bum provocatively to those inclined to be excited by the offer of the anal region. For make no mistake about it, this 'lady' knows the powerful attraction of this part of the anatomy to the dogs who pursue her, sniffing the air expectantly—and, on occasion, shoving their noses up the anus itself, on reaching milady's boudoir. Doubt not the degraded antics of your man, and woman, about-town. Such specialties are common, though unknown to the unsuspecting naiveté of the average, well-meaning do-gooder.

Our trollope, though impeded by her practice of chewing gum with her mouth open, manages to leer satisfactorily at most males in her vicinity, in the promise of unimaginable delights to come. Sex is not on offer; that is expressly forbidden, being replaced by practices so far removed from the innocence of natural sex that the term simply does not apply. A 'dirty good time' is what is sought, and the less it has to do with sexuality, the more satisfying it is. Bold as brass, and exhibiting an unmistakable pride in her infamy, Madame Pompadour saunters down the thoroughfare in the sure knowledge of an eventual pick-up. And it is not long in coming.

A bald headed, pot-bellied member of the opposite gender approaches her, and indicates his intentions right from the start by grabbing one of her ample buttocks.

Introductions having thus been effected, the couple are in haste to find somewhere to indulge their illicit anticipations. The usual place behind the cinema dustbins is out, because there is a policeman patrolling the area, and all the accommodating doorways are occupied by couples engaged in the same pursuit, condoms being flung out in every direction, having served their purpose, and being squelched underfoot by passers-by. After some time, with anticipatory spunk running down their legs, our hero and heroine fetch up, somewhere in Camden Town, in her foetid and stinking digs. The odour serves to excite the male even more, and he fully expects, as is probably the case, that his paramour has neglected to wash herself for at least a week, in the hope of enhancing the nuptials. Dog and bitch next turn themselves to the business in mind.

Anyone who doubts the common occurrence of such things is in dire need of education in the depravity of his fellow human beings. Anything goes, and if they could eat each other's' shit without it killing them, they would. This story is based on countless anecdotes related to the author, over the years, by his acquaintances, who in many cases were boasting of their exploits. Personal observation, and an instinctive understanding of humanity, are an additional source.

Representing the worst characteristics of our basically

depraved society, Romeo and Juliet decide to celebrate their infamous identification with the common herd by making it 'a night to remember'.

Sitting astride her chair, wearing only the scantiest attire, she opens her legs as widely as possible—at a hundred and eighty degrees, in fact—beckoning, indeed commanding, her lover to her, though not immediately. In order to savour the moment to the utmost, in all its disgusting implications, they stare each other in the eye, egging each other on, with the indicated fanny being the principle object of attention, and the ultimate goal of both their desires. It takes on an exaggerated role, entirely dissociated from the rest of the body—apart from the bum and tits, of course—essential accessories—and, long before its destined crescendo, it is receiving the most intense stimulation, attended with assiduous devotion by Romeo's predatory hand. His first approach is to administer some butter—Sainsbury's best—to the pulsating organ in order to facilitate his eventual entry, and also to add fuel to the already raging fire. These experiences are only, in a minor way, registered on a physical basis; of far more importance is the psychological meaning, to wit, "Let us be as dirty as possible; we will reduce all decency, all nobility—all dignity—to the utmost degradation—entirely for the sake of it, and expressly because it has nothing to do with sex".

The conversation between them involves the filthiest terms imaginable—the dirtier the better—specifically designed to raise them to a frenzy. Pointing in a lewd fashion to that thing down below, she announces, in a tone calculated to goad him on, "My pussy loves meat," The indicated morsel of meat receives, from this, the greatest gratification. I have it on reliable authority—straight from the horse's mouth—*that such things are commonplace.*

At one time you could tell a whore straight off; she probably had cock-struck eyes—an unmistakable sign—permanently protruding on stalks, or, alternatively, swollen to the size of golf balls. The strange fact is that you hardly ever see it nowadays, probably because the illusion that caused it has now been dispelled by the overwhelming frequency with which it appears in today's society; it has achieved such widespread acceptance as being the norm, *that it has actually come to be no longer unreal. Reality itself has succumbed to this all-pervading madness; the most innocent-looking girls are probably the most dedicated tarts.* I am no longer fooled by the universal belief that most people are innocent; at a rough guess, I would say at least seventy-five per cent of Western civilization is sworn to evil—giving them the benefit of the doubt; it is probably even more. Scratch a nice girl, and you will find a whore; married whores are the worst, even though they may reserve their iniquity for their husbands—purely because they are so used to his response that they get an even greater thrill out of disgracing the marriage-bed than defiling the many beds of promiscuity.

Once again, I must insist that everything I say about modern man and woman is unreservedly true, in every sordid detail. I have not travelled the underground way for nothing, man's sheer evil having forced itself on me at every step. A morass of wanton wickedness lies around every corner, and within every heart.

Preliminary to the actual act of intercourse, the happy couple demonstrate their high regard for each other by getting into a highly unconventional clinch, whereby the female crouches over her lover, presenting him with a privileged view of the area between her genitals and her anus; this is commonly known as 'the bivet'—"If that goes, the lot drops", (I was informed of this particular delectation by one very practiced in all things to do with the degradation of the body, so I do not doubt his word). The response of the male is optional; he can either shove his nose up her cunt, or shove it up her arse, taking care not to dislodge the bivet. Either of these options is acceptable to the expectant female.

Following this diverting foreplay, our lovers finally decide to proceed to the stage of sexual intercourse, which is after all the object. Adopting the anal-presentation position, that being deemed the rudest, especially when exaggeratedly displayed, Juliet discourages her suitor from 'putting it up her arse', on the grounds that her fanny is more urgently disposed—on this occasion. Introducing his member into the required place, Romeo is tempted to shoot his lot there and then— 'premature ejaculation', as Mary Whitehouse says—but anticipating this, Juliet reprimands him in advance, being desirous of prolonging the act for a decent amount of time so she can savour its dirtiness to the full. In this conflict of interests, where Romeo is trying to get it off as soon as possible, and Juliet is attempting to prolong her very decided satisfaction, the two partners reach an uneasy compromise; "If you promise to shag the living daylights out of me—without relent—I will, in return, administer a 'sixty-nine' to you—when we have recovered". On receipt of such an offer, what else could Romeo do but raise such a gallop that his arse was going like a fiddler's elbow, and such was his ardour that his cock nearly emerged from his sweetheart's mouth. But, duty done, and Juliet well and truly shagged, he was finally awarded the long-awaited attentions of her mouth. Whether she actually bit him or not, I don't know, because she usually kept this treat for her more demanding clients, but having to make do with second best, our hero nevertheless succeeded in attaining a fairly satisfactory orgasm—and Juliet swallowed the lot.

Divine Form

I once heard a man describe woman's breasts as 'jutting elasticity'. Not all women have 'juttingly elastic' breasts, which at least suggests that they aren't absolutely essential; but I wish to say that, in love—or in the act of love—the elasticity is only prominent in the most heated moments, just as the jutting male genitals only achieve their explicit appearance— or meaning—also in the most heated moments, <u>when all is revealed in extremis</u>.

The heated moments may or may not last a long time, but, <u>in the finality of those moments, the elasticity disappears, leaving only Man and Woman</u>, in knowledge of each other— not of any 'elasticity'.

Who, after all, would want to be valued for his, or her, 'jutting elasticity'?

*   *   *

In the art class we see, not bodily form, but Divine Form; there is no sexuality here—that is left at the door. And so, in the bedroom—the chamber of the Spiritual (or Divine) Body. Sexuality there is, but Olympian sexuality—the sex of the Gods: those who know how to make love with love; pleasure, yes—abundantly—but all that melts in the Final Moment.

*   *   *

Pleasure is the means of sex, love is the purpose of sex.

*   *   *

So all's well that ends well, and, as Freud would say, "One good shag deserves another"; so I have no doubt that Romeo and Juliet will encounter each other again along some dark alley, and, who knows, they might be so inspired by each other's company as to attempt a performance in public?

On their later, and more elaborate, return to sexual union we observe perhaps the most fundamental fact about illicit sex: its masturbatory nature. The illusion that masturbation essentially is, becomes conveyed in the following account.

The ultimate experience, or sensation, of the whore—in fact her defining purpose—is that of being shagged to death. Within this much-desired annihilation—a total perversion of that experienced by the good whore—her most earnest wish is for a terminating dissolution into nothingness, a universal conflagration, herself at the centre, where everything in Creation is destroyed, including God himself, and all representation of decency, honour, and self-respect; truly the end of the civilized and conscious world; this is Whoredom. All sense, even, of self is dissolved, and the final result is a flood of frenetic spunk ejaculated from both organs, leaving the participants satisfied by their enormity, yet not having encountered any shame whatever beyond their intention to destroy any recognition that such a thing exists.

"Shag me until the rivers run with blood," she cries

fervently. And they do. Night is wrought down upon the face of the earth, and in our hellion's frantic imagination, legions of unspeakable horrors are unleashed in the name of Lust. Mother's devotion, and Father's fond indulgence, are deliberately desecrated as the chief symbols of respect itself. In many orgiastic revels, the memory of parental example is pissed upon, and farted upon—all of this literally, and with the greatest delight. Rushing madly around the venue, men and women cavort in a grotesque dance, committing every conceivable outrage, even to the involvement of stinking faeces.

This is the reality of illicit sex; the only alternative in a loveless world. This is what your daughters, and your sons, get up to when your back is turned. Do not doubt it.

Towards this destructive goal, all masturbation is directed—even the least evil—beginning with adolescents; adolescents are perhaps the most unbridled exponents, and probably that section of society where orgies are most likely to break out. Nine times out of ten, it is on these occasions that illegitimate babies are conceived, among the sprawling bodies of children hell-bent on rending down the very meaning of Innocence. Sperm-spattered carpets and soiled bathtubs greet the eye of the returning parent. And this infamy, this untold wickedness—flouted specifically in the face of society—is the very thing that is so feverishly sought; purely for the sake of being, and doing, evil.

This is, I am afraid to say, an instinct—an instinct within every human being. *Original, and innate, sin is an undoubted fact: man is born evil.* Even that new-born babe can become a raging whore—by her own will. Innocence is a very paradoxical thing, containing the greatest wickedness in full potentiality from the very first moment that man was created. The state of Unity, or primitivism, though it may be innocent, is eminently susceptible to perversion. The only innocence that in fact it has, is endowed by God in his forgiveness, knowing that primitive man, *having no individuality*, is moved entirely by the Collective Will, and, ultimately, cannot be held responsible. However, in civilization, *which is built upon the responsibility of the citizen*, there is no excuse for wrongdoing.

By its very nature, masturbation is concerned with illusion; that is its essential character, and its unavoidable purpose. Kids, and even adults, 'abuse' themselves in the true meaning of the word; not only is this practice devoid of reality—a fantasy, by definition, falling short of the objective fact—but it also involves immature sexuality and the deliberate attempt, as a result, to reduce the sexual experience to something sordid. In this, wankers invariably succeed. While masturbation may be necessary, or, at least, unavoidable, in the early years of youthful experience, it is perpetuated far beyond its intended period; in fact, in most men, it persists until death—*expressly so within intercourse.* The illusion that the woman in front of you accords to the hussy in your fantasy, leads you to abuse not only yourself but, at the same time, your unfortunate lover. *You have never even seen a woman.*

Blindly ploughing his furrow, the average man dishonours his wife nightly, the long-suffering victim sacrificing herself on the altar of 'conjugal rights'. But, in addition to the illusion that the objective woman is the one in your fantasies, we observe the further number of illusions contained in the gross immaturity of the fantasy itself. *With exaggerations and dissociations applied to every limb, the lover's body is dismembered.* In the mind of this raging reprobate, even as he ploughs his way forward, arm is rent from leg, tit is rent from arse, and arse is rent from head; and all are rent from the body itself. What we are left with is a butcher's shambles. So undeveloped is this man's sexuality, that he fastens upon whatever limb, or aspect, of the body appears to him, and proceeds to fuck it. An arse, in particular, is one of the most popular morsels—the fatter the better (he can at least see that much). In stuffing his poor wife's body—or part of her body—it is a small mercy that he doesn't actually 'shove it up her arse'; but this is probably because, in his warped mind, he dimly realizes that the woman herself has somehow to respond—*so that he can have the satisfaction of finally disgracing her*; after all, if she joins you in your personal degradation, your desires are doubly fulfilled,— especially as this would serve to confirm the belief that your wife actually is a whore. Even a whore, however, in Lothario's mind, only exists as a collection of severed parts, which, somehow, are supported in a semblance of the female presence by the spirit of whoredom itself, which manages to maintain an existence without having a body. My Stepmother has expressed the enterprising wish to set up a business selling inflatable women; she should have a roaring success.

Symbolic in the arse is sex; symbolic in the tits is heart; symbolic in the head is spirit. These three elements of the total sexual experience should work together, thus uniting the body in its rightful innocence.

*   *   *

<u>Imagination And All</u>

Imagination doesn't just <u>know</u> all; it <u>is</u> all.

*   *   *

Think your whole being into every drop of sperm.
Every drop contains you.
You <u>are</u> contained within every drop.
Seek it
—Seek yourself within.
Within and without—
There rests all.

*   *   *

It is not pleasure that drives us,
Nor a dwelling in ugliness,
But simply the innocence of Beauty
—Simply Innocence,
And never does she display herself
In any unfortunate attitude

*   *   *

Our unfortunate heroine assaults her own self-respect for the very purpose of *losing* self-respect. *The end result of Freud's and psychiatry's demonic attentions is precisely this: all whores, all teenage tarts, and all married jades, take, as their sexual remit, the explicit intention to destroy all semblance of self-respect. So intent are they on reducing all Creation to nullity, that the one thing, above all, they desire, is the sensation of being totally without respect for themselves.* So attractive is this tumultuous experience, that every woman and child rushes madly towards it. Pants and bras are discarded as hastily as possible, the scene of the crime being immaterial even if it exposes them to public view. The back seat of a car, a prickly hay-loft, or the school broom-cupboard—the more mean and disreputable it is, the more it contributes to the essential feeling of disgrace—of disgracing, and of being disgraced. *The whore is sworn to shit herself into perdition, carrying all babes, all innocents, along on the effluent tide. And the Devil receives her, laughing, in his lair.* 'Your soul-mate, Lucifer, stokes the fire upon which is immolated the most precious endowment to issue from your Maker: *the sense of shame— yes, inhibition—designed to protect your sense of Self from the very degradation you seek to immerse it in. Face to face stand Self and its own desire to dissolve into nothing.*

And this is the point:-

Within this Self-respect is held the essence of Individuality.

The sense of self is created, consciously, by civilization, in its process of individuation. Yes, selfhood exists in primitivism: it protects it. But in the primitive mentality, selfhood is totally unconscious, and has nothing to do, except potentially, with individuality. Nevertheless, when individuality later arises in the civilized, or conscious, world, the first thing it calls upon is a sense of self; it supports the self, it is supported *by* the self; and this sense of self originates in the deep unconscious of primitive man.

Innocence, whether primitive or civilized, being represented and protected by the instinct of self-respect, is the first target of man's evil—man's instinctive evil. Instinct against instinct. The potential destruction even in natural, or primitive, man would nevertheless not find expression unless it came up against civilized culture, which would provoke it into action. Natural man, therefore, is innocent, as a new-born babe sleeping unaware of the destructive forces latent within its breast. Civilization is a profoundly regrettable thing, yet it is necessary—*it is man's destiny*; and it cannot, by the demands of evolution, afford to be reversed.

The instinct to destroy that which thou art, is the curse of consciousness and civilized culture. Consciousness—including the consciousness of self—is what is under threat. And what threatens it is Instinct itself, the original, unconscious Unity.

The all-out war between consciousness and unconsciousness, or civilization and nature, has been in progress ever since the Western world broke into history. For Eastern civilization was not founded on the suppression of Nature; only in the West has there arisen the extroverted mentality necessary to subject the world of Instinct. Through its defining function, physical science, extroversion, or the outward-oriented psyche, has grasped its own, instinctive self by the throat, and throttled the life out of it, and now we wonder why Instinct has reacted.

In the person of the Whore, Instinct has risen up and bitten us on the arse. We are our own worst enemy. The Whore herself, whether good or bad, is innocent, and, ultimately, the involuntary instrument of Western man's own psyche. However outrageous she may be, she is still Woman, natural, and responding only to Nature. Her only sin, in fact, is in destroying herself; that is her final goal, and Creation is roped in to achieve that end; can we blame anyone for committing suicide to escape the intolerable truth?—*The truth being that the burden of civilization is too heavy to endure*.

*   *   *

And so, all whores are pardoned and forgiven.

Now, the story of Christ—and *his* Whore. Christ's Whore—and let us be sure what we are talking about—is, simply, Woman, whether primitive or civilized; and knowing the plight, the dire state, into which his Woman has been plunged, as a result of the collision between Consciousness and Instinct, he has hastened to earth to find her and to rescue her. Woman herself, being of course Mother as well as Whore, and also both a civilized and primitive creature, experiences in full all these identities, but it is the evil nature of the femme-fatale that Christ is here to address—in no uncertain manner.

Christ has always been passionately in love with his wayward adventuress—even to her most extreme obscenities—so much so that he has pursued her all his life in lurid fantasy—lurid because of the Whore's nature, not his own. *Christ remains innocent.* For all the appalling experiences he has undergone, in search of her—many of which have even been caught, on camera, unknown to himself at the time—the devoted Lover emerges unscathed. I have no doubt that, upon the appearance of those scandalously-obtained images, on the television and in the press—and this undoubtedly will take place, such is man's hatred for his Creator—there will arise a wave of universal condemnation and ridicule. *He is a martyr to the world of physical appearances.* For nothing could in fact be more obviously untrue.

Nevertheless, despite the truth of it, humanity is so set within physical existence that it cannot penetrate the barriers of visible form. *This is probably one of Christ's most important messages—specifically presented in the guise of pornographic material, and designed, in fact, to look the opposite of what it actually is. Look beneath the surface.*

The extreme of love that your Lord bears for his wanton mistress, should never be questioned, for within it lies the truth about the Lord himself, *and also the means of his resurrection.* The only hope that Christ has of being depositioned from his lifelong Cross, rests with man himself. Only man can release his own Saviour. Until Christ's absolute innocence is recognized, he will remain condemned to Ridicule; as far as he is concerned, there is no more terrible a crucifixion.

Who, in fact, do you see in those farcical images? Is it Jesus Christ—or is it you, yourself?

In coming to earth, after two thousand years, Christ appeared in the figure of Anthony Hill. A rather unlikely name—it has no significance—but Anthony Hill was once recognized as the Messiah forty-five years ago. He was famous, and courted for his celebrity. But five years later, disaster befell him, and, ever since, his identity has been withdrawn. This was the true beginning of his crucifixion. From then on, he has been subjected to every conceivable form of abuse, the worst of which has probably been that of ridicule. Your Lord's very dignity—the last quality remaining to him—was first snatched from him in those scurrilous films peddled from one hotel screen to another.

But the Lord himself set up the whole thing. From his birth onwards it was fated that he would one day take upon himself the task of *instructing mankind in the reality of the universe surrounding him*. And the first thing to learn about the physical universe, is that it is a total illusion. The universe exists only in God's mind; the universe *is* mind. Any physical reality it may have is bestowed by the Lord from his godhead, and however incontrovertible a physical fact may appear to be, it is dispersed into nothing by the permeating ether of the Universal Psyche. Hence, when you look at a turd of shit, just remember that its reality does not lie in its stink, but very probably in the lily contained within its fathomless depths.

But the fantasies themselves, that Christ employed in such desperate pursuit of his beloved, were, quite frankly, enough to make your hair curl. Your own Saviour possesses, in fact, the most depraved imagination in the history of mankind. How does this come about?

Alongside his obscenity, Christ manifests the most beautiful, noble, and loving fantasies that have ever been devoted to woman. Where, then, has he gone wrong?

Given that the Lord so loves his Creation,

represented quintessentially by Woman, that he has come to earth to save it, what is the most likely thing he would do? He would first of all *sympathize*. And, sympathizing, he would, again given his nature, propel himself into an emotional involvement with his creatures—even to the point of identifying himself with their all-too evident evil. Truly a state of martyrdom inspired by absolute love.

Oats and Whey

She and I—
A cocktail of masculine and feminine,
Love and hate—to be expunged-
Oats and whey,
Mixed in a porridge of flesh and essence,
Turned out in the Body
Pure and untainted.
Yea and Nay,
Advance and response
But never rebuff
And finally, Good and Evil,
The pith of all;
Adam and Eve,
Innocence disposed,
Then lost,
—Then found again:
Paradise Lost, Paradise Regained
—Milton, so old and wise—
Parsifal by any other name.
All this in She and I:
Body come, body go:
Abuse to be avoided
—Look only into her lovely eyes.

*   *   *

Sex is You:
All those unravelling forces within;
None bad, only innocent—
If you allow innocence to be innocence.
No pigs allowed here,
Only beauty.
Do it <u>for</u> her

Added to this display of compassion, is the Lord's crippling reluctance to carry out his further mission on earth, which is to punish and condemn all wrong-doing. Rather than wield his Father's authority, he has given way to his instinctive feelings, and sacrificed his own life, innocence, and the right to happiness, by rolling in the gutter for most of his terrestrial existence. But this very lifelong trauma was the basis, whether or not by design, of Christ's, or Parsifal's, enlightenment. Passing practically all his working life in troglodyte kitchens, he has lived close to the seam of underground communication, and led by his self-destructive tendencies, coupled with his consuming passion for the Whore, the shambling pot-man was, almost despite himself, educated in the subliminal life of the metropolis. The knowledge thus produced could not have been gained in any other way. Identifying himself with evil, the Lord *became* evil; and this is the fate of any prophet who cares enough for his people to undertake a personal odyssey, into hell, on their behalf.

Ever since, indeed, he has believed himself to be the most evil man on earth—which is, perhaps, appropriate, considering his identity—an inevitable consequence of his self-submission. And his gutter-seeking desperation has only, thereby, been increased. Walking, or attempting to walk, down the street, his most urgent wish is to vanish into one of the rat-holes in the pavement. His sordid fantasies, though indeed impelled by love, have done nothing to increase his self-esteem, and he fears, mightily, every day of his life, that the evidence will be betrayed in his eyes. So, the Pariah of creation—stranded, so far without hope, in the centre of his own universe—awaits deliverance. Until very recently, he had not even that hope, being forced to pursue a life of sheer aggression, and not much else, accompanied by his fellow desperadoes in the Legion of the Damned, condemned to fighting until they were stopped by a merciful bullet. The only hope they did have, was to die fighting—their sole expiation. And thus, all those gallant souls, with only their courage to commend them, who, over the last hundred and fifty years, entered the ranks of the fabled Foreign Legion, faced a life without any hope except the final release in death. Well, let me, here and now, establish the record of their undying glory. Distributed over the many battlefields of North Africa, under the merciless sun, the debris of your sons', and lovers', last ill-fated encounters remains evident to the present day, acknowledged only by the silent tribute of the sands. Gone, probably without trace in the memory of their loved-ones, these were truly "Men with nothing to lose".

And Christ himself was their commanding officer. So he continues today, having miraculously survived death, and with the prospect of the resurrection of his self-respect before him; a resurrection administered by the welcoming heart of his waiting Muse, who is in place to draw out his long-dormant creative powers, among them the ability to love absolutely, and with the utmost purity. His self-respect will be returned to him with the re-emergence of innocence, and the truth of his supposed infamy will be established.

There are numerous other factors in Christ's 'sex-life'. First of all, this alleged 'sex-life' actually has nothing to do with sex; its apparent involvement with sex issues purely and simply from his obsession with his errant sweetheart; wherever she goes, he follows; the dirtier she becomes, the more devoted he is to her fantasies: *they are not his fantasies—they are her's.* And to get inside her, to understand her, he has to take on her characteristics. This is the true meaning of 'empathy'—and its purpose. *The distressing images, then, that you see on those screens, are the Whore herself, not Christ.* Judge not as ye would not be judged.

Other causes of the Lord's erotic behaviour include his incredibly severe physical exhaustion, which, in itself, is enough to engender a need for purely physical relief—not sexual relief. In similar fashion, his crashing physical, and mental, tension leads to the same end. The acute anxiety from which he has also suffered abominably, adds to all his other physical and mental afflictions to produce an overwhelming desire for some bodily expression; *the fact, moreover, that Christ is bodily dead, should inform you of his crying necessity to experience some form of life.* Furthermore, as he is actually suspended from both life and death—being caught in between—is it impossible to conceive of a being in such an extreme that he takes whatever recourse he can to achieve a semblance of life? And a semblance is all it is, since Christ is not even allowed to experience an orgasm. So his 'satisfaction' is actually nil. The Living-Death of which Christ's crucifixion consists, is very real.

The fantasies themselves are extreme—partly because, in order to achieve the impossible orgasm, he is forced to employ every powerfully-charged psychological impulse to that end, and, unfortunately, he never succeeds, thus remaining in a permanently frustrated condition. This, however, is not sexual frustration, but the failure to achieve purely physical relief from a totally physical problem. The constant physical stress, therefore, is obvious, and a more diabolical torture was never devised by God.

Desperately pursuing life, or his Whore, and at the same time doing his best to destroy himself, Christ is in a bloody mess! If he ever recovers, no-one will be more surprised than himself.

*　　*　　*

THE PSYCHOLOGY OF PLEASURE

In analysing the psychology of pleasure itself, we are obviously dealing, at the same time, with the psychology of the Whore. I had assumed there was a difference, and to a certain extent there is, but inevitably I shall have to treat them as one. Of course the Whore as a person is distinct from the mere experience of pleasure, though I have defined her as 'the woman who experiences pleasure', or even as, simply, 'pleasure'. The difference, or similarity, is significant. Pleasure itself, taken as a physical sensation, has no personal connotation and I want to make it absolutely clear that, under no circumstances, would I even contemplate the recommendation of pleasure on the basis of mere sensation.

Pleasure and Sacrifice

Pleasure must be sacrificed to love—first sacrificed, then found again within love. But you cannot approach a woman from the point of view of pleasure: she will fade before your eyes.

* * *

If you look at a girl with pleasure, you won't see her.

Unfortunately, it is on this very basis that pleasure is recommended by psychiatry, which should know better. But having studied the school of Freud for most of my life—at a distance, I may say—I have seen, quite beyond doubt, that its scientific foundation has led to horrendous inroads on the moral welfare of the Western world in general. Thanks to the arrogance, and ignorance, of the scientific body, sexual pleasure has been denuded of all personal meaning. Reduced not only to a physical sensation, but to an exclusively genital sensation at that, sexuality has lost its primary purpose, which is, of course, to furnish man and woman with the means of loving each other. I know it is 'old hat' to talk of love, and spirit, and 'all that', but in subtracting these things from the sexual equation, you actually destroy it. Taking their sexual morality, indeed their whole sexual education, from their nightly absorption in 'Sex Parade' instead of consulting their sense of self-respect—which they do not possess anyway—the troglodytes who make up the bulk of the British population have been left with the aesthetic awareness of a bunch of mountain gorillas. The nationally-approved exhibition of shouting and shagging—'Sex Parade'—is received uncritically in every squalid sitting-room around the country. Grandma and Grandad, Ma and Pa, and all the little smellies, are congregated around the telly, stuffing their faces with chips and scratching their privates ruminatively, as one more scene from the 'soap' comes up, with the heroine, dressed salaciously, of course, draping herself over the bed. Ensconced in the bed expectantly—and I will say they don't actually show his chopper—the hero at once shoves his hand up the girl's pants, on the assumption that the less circumspection he shows, the more she will like it— which is in fact the case. You must understand that this is only a show, and that the people involved are actors; it follows that their main purpose is to titillate the public, and to this end the producer has instructed them to 'be as dirty as possible'—with the full approval of those who run the television. From the top down, the order goes out that family entertainment should be particularly obscene: the public likes it; and what the public likes, it must certainly have. Neither the public at large, nor Mr X, nor anybody in the land will voice the slightest dissent—for the simple reason that no-one knows it *is* obscene. The media, the government—even the church—have conspired to obscure the public's sense of morality to such an extent that not one person in the country possesses any conviction. Intellectuals strive to tell us that love— and God, too—no longer exists, and agony aunts go out of their way to remind us that what a girl likes is 'uncomplicated sex'—and the hotter the better. If flowers are delivered to the door, it is but a preliminary to a really sizzling shag. Caught between illicit sex and their own, would-be conscience, British man and woman are unable to make up their minds as to whether obscenity itself is acceptable or not—or whether it exists in the first place. The whole idea of public profanity has become so overlaid with see-sawing official attitudes—not one day passing without some contradictory comment in the press—that the average punter hasn't a clue, by now, what is meant by 'sex'. The term has come to represent such a wide variety of things, most of them inconsistent, that the original sense has been completely lost. The glaringly obvious difference between a good fuck and a saintly offer of devotion entirely eludes the consciousness of everyone from the vicar to the local rapist. Consequently, we see clergymen being had up for distasteful advances, and gang-bangers being exonerated on the grounds that their sexual needs had to be expressed—the one arising from the conviction that 'sex' is innocent on all occasions, and the other being the result of Sigmund Freud's dictum that "Man was put on earth to screw". Of course, this confusion would all be cut short in a trice if the public did but once pay heed to their natural integrity; they would know immediately that evil was evil. But that is the last thing anyone wants; 'self-respect' went out with the long line of scientific denunciation from Darwin onwards. And more than that:

what lies at the bottom of this failure to voice their sense of shame *is sheer cowardice—the crawling capitulation to any show of force, whether mental or physical.* Man's weakness in the face of peer pressure is execrable. This, above all, is 'original sin'; God expects his creatures to exhibit the spunk with which they were made.

On seeing Romeo put his hand up the girl's pants, Grandad nearly has a heart-attack—it has been such a long time, you see; and Grandma can't remember when she last had a hearty back-scuttle. Memories at once come flooding back, and the junior members of the family being in a similar state of arousal, due to the irresistible performance on the screen, all restraint is abandoned, and the night evolves into a full-scale orgy.

Chips and bottles of coke are hastily pushed behind the sofa, and knickers and bras fly all over the place, accompanied by Grandma's corsets. To open the proceedings, Pa takes a run-up to Ma's waiting backside and, after a few minutes of frenetic activity on the part of the parents their youngest daughter, being quick on the uptake, contributes what by any standards would be considered a remarkable feat: standing on her head, she manages to insert the table-lamp, without the shade, of course, up her youthful orifice. This unorthodox variety of sexual procedure has been inspired by her clandestine reading of Dr Psycho's text-books, which leave one with the unmistakable impression that the female genitals are designed to receive anything that looks like a penis; to psychiatry's way of thinking, it isn't necessary to employ the genuine article, since masturbatory experiences do not demand adherence to reality—and for that reason are to be recommended.

The girl's older sister, in fact, is an expert exponent of the 'vibrator'—another inheritance from 'Women's lib', according to which men are unnecessary—which, however, she eschews on this occasion in favour of the real thing, which is not long in coming, courtesy of her brother.

This is a night to be recorded in erotic history! However, all good things come to an end, and after a prolonged session of debauchery, during which several athletic records are broken, the family eventually collapses in exhaustion, though, may I say, contentedly fucked, screwed, and shagged. Their bodies remain strewn around the sitting-room, in their various sleeping postures, until the char-lady discovers them in the morning—much to her envy.

This very scene is the desired result, and calculated effect, of the pornographic programme put out by the cast and production team of 'Sex Parade'—on any night you care to mention.

The Ultimate Secret Of Desire

The ultimate secret of desire is simply one of will: voluntary will and involuntary will.

The sacrifice of sex, or pleasure, is indeed a sacrifice, and it is no good pretending otherwise; to pretend that sex 'doesn't matter' is an illusion, and, for that reason, a false hope.

To give up sex, we have to do so voluntarily, because two contrary wills contradict each other; in other words, they fight. Positive and negative can only find resolution in co-operation; therefore, the sacrifice of desire has to be voluntary: <u>to</u> will, <u>for</u> will. Will has to free itself by an act of conscious debate: what we are talking about is <u>conscious </u>will. Desire <u>itself</u> has to be freed, and it can only be freed by being brought into the fold—tamed, realized: in other words, brought face to face with itself Facing itself, desire sees itself as illusion<u>, and the two contrary wills cancel each other out</u>.

Man has but to bring himself to be conscious of his two contrary wills: Good and Evil. But this takes a lifetime.

* * *

Rest not, for one moment, on the assumption that such a thing could not be true: the obvious intention of all such public displays of obscenity is to incite their audience to a frenzied participation. What else? Throughout history, this has been the sole and ultimate purpose of all pornography whether by photograph, film, or stage; people queue down the street for it, and entertainers are only too eager to give it. Mr X will protest in outrage that he could not possibly be guilty of such a thing, but it is implicit in every broadcast programme concerning sexual images that titillation even to the point of indulgence, should occur. Whether or not this is acknowledged consciously, it remains the deliberate aim of televised sexuality. "We all like it, therefore let us all have it, wherever and whenever."

Though it will never be acknowledged, due to the general obscuration of all sexual matters, and to the inability of the average citizen to grasp any truth whatever, the propagation of lewd and suggestive material is dependent, first of all, on the unconscious desire of society to receive it, specifically for physical gratification (though this may be only potential) and secondly, on the unconscious intention to supply it. Both the desire to receive it and the intention to supply it are, again unconsciously, *based on a mutual commitment to debauchery*; and whether or not this results in actual expression, it is the specific aim of the contract. More often than not it leads to solitary masturbation, and almost as often to intercourse, but in either case the fantasies are invariably illicit. Even if nothing ensues right there in front of the television, the images being broadcast are noted for future use in the bedroom; and you may be sure that the more lurid they are, the more welcome they are. The undiscriminating members of society are so sworn to lustful behaviour that they are not even aware of it, and if you dared to suggest this to them they would be most offended. This illogical and paradoxical reaction is the result of a complete lack of moral and aesthetic awareness, on the one hand, and of an incredible belief in their moral and aesthetic rectitude on the other. *In other words, these people don't even exist;* for existence depends on consciousness, or thought: "I think, therefore I am". Physical existence is non-existence, for the reason that the physical world is totally unconscious, and any existence that might pertain to it is entirely immersed in a collective whole; the all-absorbing 'black-hole' in which everything vanishes. Your physical appearance is just that: an illusionary fantasy. You may pinch yourself and think: "that's flesh!" But what is flesh? In reality, flesh is just an idea, a concept, a thought; *it only achieves solidity when thought itself becomes experienced.* Solidity is simply that side of life which we call 'experience'; in other words, unconscious thought, or thought brought down into the lower reaches of the mind where everything is so slow to move that it *actually looks* solid. In this area there is no perceptible movement, and consequently no time; for one's sense of time depends on the perception of movement. And if there is no time, there is no space, the two being interdependent. As the laws of physics will tell you, there can be no physical phenomenon, in other words no object, without the presence of both time and space, (and if the laws of physics do not tell you that, they should). For example, take that rock, over there: you can understand why it would need space, because, if it hadn't space, it would have no spatial extent—obviously; and without spatial extent, it simply wouldn't exist. However, assuming it *has* spatial extent, it still wouldn't exist without time; *for time enables space to exist.* How, you should ask yourself, could space exist *without something to extend it? What makes space spread?* Time was specially devised to do just that; *without it, space would be nothing but an infinitesimal point without any extent whatever.* In other words, space needs time, and time needs space; time needs space simply because, *without space, it would have nothing to extend.* In other words, it would be redundant; space was invented specifically to give time something to do: time is the great mover; space is that which is moved. A perfect partnership.

The active and passive principles find expression here; an antinomy perfectly related within itself; time being the active, space being the passive—interrelated, distinct, *yet identical*. That rock exists because of both space and time, *but it would not exist at all if they were not identified*.

Having established that the existence of flesh, or physical reality, is determined by the relationship of time and space, and having established previously that flesh is also a form of thought, it is likely that time and space themselves are basically but a thought, and it seems to me to be quite obvious that physical reality, if it has any reality at all, only exists as thought in the mind of man; again the axiom: "I think, therefore I am", which could not be replicated as "I sense, therefore I am". For sense is ruled by sense; sense knows *only* sense—and physical sense at that. It cannot see beyond itself; it cannot see. Therefore it cannot think; for seeing is thinking, and thinking, seeing.

Sense only 'knows:- I 'know' through hearing, touching, smelling, tasting and, lastly, 'seeing'; but the physical sense of 'seeing' is the direct opposite of *the mental faculty* of 'seeing', which is—thinking. Only 'knowing', then, the sensory world simply cannot compete with the mental world of thought—*or abstraction*. The sensory world is 'one'—'one', both in, and by, itself; *this world of oneness is, then, collective and, consequently, nothing within it exists: to exist, we need to abstract ourselves out of oneness, or collectivity.*

This digression was necessary for two reasons: first, to prove the utter illusion of the physical, or sensory, world, and second, to show the crying necessity for abstraction, or thought, in every aspect of our lives from sex onwards. *For, sex, or the lower reaches of Love, is the very essence of the physical-sensory world: therefore it does not exist.*

There are two aspects of the non-existence of sex: one, how to recognize its non-existence, or illusion, and two, how to overcome that illusion and possibly to rescue sex from it. In recognizing that sex is an illusion we are not necessarily enabled to remove it *from* that illusion, but we may be able to continue working *within* the illusion. On the other hand, we have the possibility, brought to us by Anthony Hill, of rescuing sex from its illusionary plight, and depositing it on the plane of the Spiritual Body.

Before I launch into a peroration on the Spiritual Body, let me just say a few pertinent words on consciousness-unconsciousness. In common with every other pair of contraries (or opposites) consciousness must *contain* unconsciousness, and unconsciousness must *contain* consciousness; it is not enough to merely 'possess an image' of the other. What they actually possess, *in their* *own soul*, is the *identity* of the other—alive and kicking. The soul (anima, animus)*³ of each contrary keeps it on the straight and narrow; in other words *it maintains it in a relationship with the other*: This is vital, because, without it, we get dissociation and exaggeration: in a word, 'obscenity'. *Without the 'presence' of each opposite within the other, we have an 'absence' of Reality: the Reality of relationship, of the Third Element, which rises far above the mere contraries, and constitutes the mind of the woman, or man, herself; which is, in fact, a combination in full of both consciousness and unconsciousness, marking, yet again, the Supra-Conscious.*

An amorous frolic does not necessarily reach the Supra-Conscious, but ideally it would. The more serious experience of total emotional annihilation, however, brought about by violation, would usually result in the most definite knowledge that you have been dissolved in your husband's love, whether or not that knowledge is conscious. Do remember that violence, in love, is an expression of tenderness.

(I shall, in fact, postpone the dissertation of the Spiritual Body until a later date.)

*   *   *

3. See C.G. Jung, Psychological Types.

AN ACCOUNT OF LOVE'S COMEDY, IN WHICH THE WHORE IS ALTERNATED WITH THE MOTHER:-

Emerging from the recent crescendo of our bodies, she relaxed, fervently, in my arms, becoming once again the dear little girl who had started it all. I had taken her on an adventure into womanhood, but, on seeing her there in all her motherly femininity, so vulnerable and open to abuse, I cried, "You darling, wonderful, little thing! What wouldn't I do for you!" Responding immediately, such was her nature, she cried in return, "Do it, then! Do it all over again!"

Pleasure and Illusion

Pleasure is an illusion except within love; outside love, pleasure is a disaster. Look within, and only then will you find.

Unless you look into my eyes, you won't see me.

*   *   *

Pleasure finds its putative reality only within love.

Pleasure blinds us to reality. Look at me with pleasure in mind, and you won't see me.

*   *   *

If you lose sight of the girl herself—her eyes, her face, her loveliness—you have lost sight of pleasure as well; for pleasure only exists within the girl's soul—to which the eyes are the gateway.

*   *   *

The two of us being roused immediately to a high old state of desire, we were soon precipitated into a very receptive condition, and she informed me, "You may do anything you like with me!" Now, what else could I do but give her the most profound pleasure I could think of? But approaching her circumspectly, I first of all kissed her, passionately, on the lips, and then worked my way down, kissing her continuously, to her wondrously beautiful young breasts. Once there, I must admit I made a meal of it, and when she thrust that gorgeous bosom towards me, imploring my devotion—a most erotic area, this—I pressed my face to it, declining, come what may, to be moved from there until the milkman called in the morning. However, one's fondest dreams are shattered, and, duty calling as ever, one must proceed further; there are areas below in greater need of attention. I desired to render her into the ripest fruit in Creation's garden— juices flowing—in the hope that she would be inspired to some highly demonstrative, and possibly rude, act. And, indeed, being in no further need of encouragement, the little thing proceeded to bend down in front of me, presenting the loveliest arse in the world. On receipt of this invitation, I approached her, maddened with the pure lust of love, and determined to give her the best bloody fucking she had ever had. Upon my entering her, she was in such a state of excitement that she uttered a little cry of sheer delight—not for the sexual content alone, but also for the joy of our personal contact. Knowing her extreme state of urgency and anticipation, I gave myself up to the most deplorable exhibition of sexual ardour that you could possibly conceive of (I am surprised Gordon Brown didn't come down and excommunicate me on the spot). Pushing it up her as far as possible, until it practically penetrated her oesophagus—wherever that is—I fucked her as hard and relentlessly as I could. She was in no doubt of what was happening to her. And that little girl, thrilling beneath me, was reduced to a quivering bundle of joy and physical ecstasy all in one frantic, interminable moment, receiving not just the utmost pleasure but, also, the most profound love that Christ, in his infinite heart, *could bestow on an essential virgin. For, Mother and Whore were never before separated, and, for that reason, never realized, or brought together.*

The Madonna and I relaxed once more in each other's arms, she, at once, the mature woman and the trembling little girl who had originally inspired me. Never once had we lost sight of the compelling factor of *giving*— the whole point of it—though, in the throes of physical pleasure, we were inevitably immersed in the wish simply to enjoy ourselves. *Nevertheless, we were conscious of her desire to provoke, and of my desire to be provoked; for without provocation, no-one is fucked, and no-one is inspired to do the fucking. She gives by provoking, and I give by fucking.*

But neither of us is *conscious* of love—that is, of the good half of it—nor do we *want* to be conscious of it. The two of us being totally unconscious of 'spiritual devotion'—though not of the heated interchange of physical 'parlance', or etiquette—my adored and abandoned little whore and I are nevertheless aware that it is being delivered—and also that we are both delivering it. Egging each other on to ever more extreme erotic demonstrations, we actually convey, by this very behaviour, our total—though unconscious—commitment to the act of love between us. In most acts of love, we move from consciousness to unconsciousness and back again, but on this occasion, where the experience was so exciting, and the 'annihilation' so intense, we were too urgently engaged to lose any time in stoking each other's passion to an immediate orgasm; nevertheless, we were very 'aware' of the heartfelt conduct of our particularly disgraceful act. The more disgraceful, the better.

It is not true to say that we are totally unconscious of giving—as opposed to 'spirit'. This paradox only becomes possible through the Subconscious, where conscious and unconscious attitudes constantly interpenetrate. No hard and fast line can be drawn between the two modes of awareness.

Revealing ourselves to each other, in our innermost nakedness—accompanied by the nakedness of our bodies—we are following out the requirements of sexual-intercourse as determined by love's first law; which is, "Bare thy souls to each other, that each of you may come to know the other absolutely".

To Conquer Desire

Make no mistake about it—desire has to be conquered—willingly.

It is, indeed, a sacrifice—*but it has to be sacrificed*. Disgust should tell you so; self-respect should tell you so; the illusion should tell you so.

Destructive fantasies are, alone, a deterrent—if seen in their true light.

*   *   *

While physical pleasure is designed not to be enjoyed for its own sake, the psychological aspect of the whole sexual experience penetrates even the thickets of pleasure for the purpose of Self-Knowledge. There could be no greater mistake than to think sex ends with pleasure; in fact, pleasure ends with sex—or with love, as it actually is. *Never judge by appearances*—the Lord's particular injunction. For the physical world—the whole of physical existence—is a complete illusion. Look right into sex, and you will discover the whole universe; take every orgasm by the throat, and submit it to examination; within that slime lies the explanation of Life, and of you and your sweetheart in particular. So treat sex with respect, and reject the call by psychology to destroy its meaning and its innocence.

You will have observed, no doubt, that the Mother and the Whore are partners, alternating in and out of our consciousness as we go from the one to the other. The Mother being spirit, and the Whore being pleasure, they are of course direct opposites, but as long as they do not actually become divorced—thus precipitating a pathological situation—they will remain in a viable relationship. Separate they must be, otherwise there would be no difference between them, *but the most singular fact about spirit and pleasure—and about the opposites in general—is that never before in history have they been consciously separated—except pathologically, when the Whore and the Mother go their disastrously dissociated ways, and cause a universal psychosis—largely through the offices of psychology itself.* The science of psychology, which was set up for the purpose of healing the breach, in man, between the opposites, has succeeded only in the perpetuation of this age-old schism, and also in such an exacerbation of it that society's neuroses have become increasingly rampant. Psychology is a liability, partly due to egotism, and partly due to the complete absence of consciousness. In failing to escape the toils of unconsciousness—the first requirement, in fact, of this science—psychology has absolutely no means of *knowing anything*, let alone the difference between lust and love; as far as psychologists are concerned, there is no difference, they put it down to 'freedom of choice'; in other words, it doesn't really matter what life-style you follow—it's all 'a matter of opinion', anyway—because human rights dictate that you are allowed to do anything; so if Joe wishes to profane the sanctity of love, and Mary Whitehouse proclaims that he is a dirty bastard, no-one has a clue who is right, the entitlement to absolute freedom—which has become the basis of our civilization—having obscured even the moral code. The judges in court are afraid to condemn anyone, and the vicars are quite likely to announce that God put us on earth to multiply, and that he doesn't actually give a fuck how we go about it. All of which was determined by Sigmund Freud a hundred years ago, and, ever since, psychology has made sure that the truth never surfaces. Unconsciousness results in ignorance, meaning that however obvious it may be, to a thinking man, that piss isn't shit—and therefore, presumably, that shit isn't piss— the descendants of Freud are convinced it is, and being oblivious of the simplest and most fundamental facts of life, they are in no position whatever to instruct the rest of us in the ways of sex. Unconsciousness itself is responsible for our inability to think, and therefore must be eradicated; psychology was put on earth to do that as a preliminary to any healing process—in fact the healing process consists precisely of the eradication of unconsciousness—but in that task it has failed abysmally, the final legacy of Freudianism being the perversion of the thinking faculty.

The opposites being on the verge of separation, as a result of the consciousness presented by my coming, spirit and pleasure, as two of those opposites, will achieve separation also. But they cannot be separated *without* consciousness—though they can be dissociated, as we witness daily in the predations of illicit sex. In the history of sexuality, it has never yet come about that the Mother and the Whore have been offered as two distinct entities. Insofar as the Whore has been given any recognition at all as a viable and innocent conception, it is solely on the basis that she is confined to the bedroom, while the Mother is confined to the kitchen, going about her matronly duties. Never do they meet. Although the Whore, according to this conception, is officially regarded as 'innocent', that merely means that sex itself has come to be accepted by society, and therefore, because anything that is accepted by society automatically becomes conventional, the Whore has received recognition as 'something necessary'—even 'desirable'. But, isolated as she is in the bedroom, away from the Mother, the problem has not been solved; we are still faced with a pathological situation: the Mother downstairs in the kitchen, kept well away from sex, and the Whore upstairs in the boudoir, conducting sexual relations on her own. This is simply impossible; the Whore needs the Mother, and the Mother needs the Whore—otherwise no sexual relations are possible.

The situation as it stands—being the direct result of Freud's thinking—means that the Whore is far from innocent—in fact she remains every bit the dirty bitch she always was; in her isolation she is the very woman ensconced at this moment in the bed of the local brothel. And unless you consider, as does every psychiatrist, that even prostitutes are innocent—simply because they practice sex, and sex, according to Freud, can never be dirty—you presumably cannot accept this state of affairs.

The Whore and the Mother must come together in one bed, the mother to do the giving and the Whore to do the receiving. You cannot have a satisfactory shag if there is no-one to donate the shagging, on the one hand, and no-one to experience the shagging on the other—unless you do the job yourself in solitary masturbation, which, unfortunately, is usually the case even during intercourse. The use of the 'vibrator' obviates the necessity of employing a male, so a whore can remain a whore even when under the unlikely impression that she is at the same time a mother; this lack of distinction being apparently what persuades people like Sally and Fanny to recommend the use of such an instrument. And so, after watching the nightly instruction on the B.B.C., half the women in Britain retire to bed with the latest version of the vibrator stuck up their fannies—husbands, redundant, forced to toss themselves off in the bathroom.

However, assuming there are some decent people left in the world, my personal recommendation is that you should first of all learn how to love, and from that will follow the ability to *make* love. Obvious, you say; but have you observed most couples in bed?

Dance of the Seven Veils

Pleasure is an illusion that only finds reality by virtue of love—as we know. But what we didn't know, was <u>the reality of reality. An illusion is an illusion, and not something real by another name</u>. Grasp this, and you are home and dry.

For, an illusion is destructive, and is only undestructive when faced with the reality that saves it. An illusion is <u>never</u> real; the only reality is when destruction no longer exists.

Illusions within illusions... Delilah dances 'The Seven Veils' until the seventh veil reveals the ultimate reality. The 'Seven Pillars of Wisdom' are constructed upon Delilah's dance; that last flimsy garment is cast aside to display the Holy of Holies.

*   *   *

The eighth, and ultimate, reality is a consistent number throughout metaphysics, from the 'Seven Pillars of Wisdom' to the eight stages of the consciousness of man; the seventh pillar gives way to the eighth, and final, revelation, whereas the eighth stage of consciousness is the final one in both instances. The Absolute Consciousness is God himself.

*   *   *

Even if they are genuinely in love, it does not follow that they are able to make love, the problem being, of course, the age-old collision of opposites, represented by spirit and earth, or pleasure. Although you may be genuinely in love, that does not mean you love sufficiently, or in the right way, to take that woman in your arms and give her 'what for'—to make her *feel* loved. No woman will feel loved by a man who cannot dominate her; she expects to be taken, not appealed to. Mary Whitehouse may be a very nice woman, but I am willing to bet she has never been properly fucked—hence her niceness, and in her tea-time conversations with the Archbishop, the two of them balancing their cups very genteelly on their knees, she will undoubtedly impart to that very worthy man the fruits of her distinct lack of experience between the bed-sheets. And the Archbishop, who, as we know, is markedly under endowed, will not advance any evidence of his undoubted passion for this benighted woman. No stirrings will occur beneath that unmanly skirt. The two of them, making sheep's eyes at each other, and not much else, will, like many other couples, be content with a platonic relationship even if they get as far as the bedroom. It is indeed possible to engage in sexual intercourse on a platonic, or almost platonic, basis. So lacking in ardour is the love-making that it is hardly worth making in the first place, and the

Archbishop is the ideal exponent (I don't think he even takes his socks off). The woman in receipt of this laggardly display of affection, if she herself has anything about her, will of course be dismayed, for all women need to feel fire in their loins; in the first place, there is no satisfaction without it, and in the second place, there is certainly no fun. How many women go to sleep at night wondering why there isn't any life in their husbands? This country is full of such curmudgeons, who apparently think woman is there to be courted by a knight-errant who keeps his cock in his trousers.

Depriving you of the uninspiring spectacle of the Archbishop actually on the job, I shall turn now to the opposite case in point: the overindulgence in pleasure. If pleasure receives too much emphasis, it is invariably because it has become too distant from its opposite, spirit; whether this distance is comparatively near or a lot further off, makes no difference; it results in a dissociation of the two functions, meaning that the aforementioned pathological event has occurred. The Mother goes on a prolonged visit to the vicar, and the whore takes up residence in the brothel; and the couple disporting themselves on the bed, while they may be enjoying a great deal of pleasure, will wake up the next morning overcome with guilt—or not, as the case may be.

Ideally, Mother and Whore would alternate in the

consciousness of the two lovers, first, perhaps, visiting the experience of pleasure—even to an extreme extent— with a minimum of interference from spirit. It is impossible to say, in each individual case, how long, or how far, one is submerged in pleasure; but even if one is submerged to the point of being unconscious of spirit, that does not mean one is unaware of it *unconsciously*; nor does it mean that you have ceased to *give* pleasure to your beloved. For she is still your beloved, however abandoned she may be to the throes of physical experience; indeed, the more unconscious she is of what is going on, the more joyful you may be inclined to feel—depending on how much you love her. For, after all, it is love we are talking about: "pleasure is love, and love pleasure—*and love the only thing that ennobles it*". This last equivocating addition speaks volumes; we are not dealing just with the two opposites, love and pleasure. Far and above that, *we are dealing with Love itself*: the Third Element, present *within* both opposites, *between* both opposites, *rising infinitely further than* the two opposites, and also *wrapping itself round and about* those opposites. And, in fact, in the final moment of climax, all semblance of both spirit and pleasure vanishes, leaving Love alone—pure, everlasting, and triumphant.

It is to be acknowledged that, in that same moment of climax, spirit and pleasure remain, to the extent that they both have to be experienced—*until consciousness takes over*. And when consciousness takes over, the reality of the opposites becomes apparent—seen to be the expression of Love itself within their most essential being, servants absolutely, and, thus exposed, they dissolve naturally into Reality, where opposites both exist and don't exist; where life and death themselves dissolve into the Eternal Present.

All this can be seen in the consciousness of love.

Inner and Outer

But the most critical secret of all is Inner-and-Outer. We have the obverse and converse sides of a coin: spirit, the inner, or outer; pleasure, the outer, or inner. Paradox, you see; for obverse is either inner or outer—or neither; converse is either outer or inner—or neither; depending on how you look.

Flip the coin over, and outer becomes inner, inner becomes outer. Love is the Third Element, pleasure and spirit being merely opposites—interchangeable and non-entities. Where we are going wrong is in affording them too much attention. As mere opposites, they are both illusions, and consequently they do not pose any threat to Love; Love is not one of the contested parties, being the only reality—pleasure and spirit knowing no reality whatever—outside the coin, or Love itself. The whole is more—a great deal more—than the sum of its parts. The coin represents the physical world; Love represents the Spiritual Body, being abstracted from the coin, or carnal body. As we know, the physical, or carnal world does not exist, and therefore has no claim on a free man. If you wish to be free, you have only to Love.

Nevertheless, if you choose, you may remain in physicality; nothing is obligatory; carnality is a gift not to be abused.

*   *   *

You have a choice; I haven't; I am bound, by my own self-destruction, to remain within the carnal world which I invented, and, therefore, to love. I would die for it—for you. And I do.

The only thing that can save me is the love—and respect—of the most exceptional woman in the world—failing my own self-respect, which I have sacrificed in a lunatic adventure in love for an undeserving world. Misplaced love has damned its Creator.

*   *   *

The whore represents unconsciousness, the mother represents consciousness. From that, all follows. The whore is experience, Nature, and unity; the mother is mentality, Civilization, and Union. The mother unites, the whore endures the opposites, in her unconscious Unity; the mother sees the opposites, from her conscious vantage-point, the whore *knows* the opposites in her unconscious den. They need each other, they honour each other; *and they both together produce the Resurrected Woman.* Dragging the suffering whore from her state of interrupted Unity, the mother rescues her by her powers of Union; the whore heals the mother, however, by providing the substance to her unifying consciousness; without the substance, the mother remains a little girl. The Resurrected Woman, therefore, rises from the ashes of the dead woman of yesteryear, mummified in her Unity.

*   *   *

A woman is two things: the Mother and the Whore. I will make every woman in the world a woman for the first time. No-one in history has known the difference between spirit and pleasure; they have never become explicit before, being identical, in a state of unity.

People have certainly *experienced* the difference between the opposites, but they have never been conscious of it; therefore they have never known either explicit spirit or explicit pleasure—*and, therefore, they have not lived.*

Although woman has, of course, been woman, she has never been a woman consciously; therefore she will become a woman for the first time. In the state of unconsciousness, no-one exists: "I am conscious, therefore I am".

Consciousness and unconsciousness: the alternation from the one to the other during the sexual experience. During the desired absence of consciousness, in the absolute abandonment to pleasure, both woman and man are essentially *aware* in their unconscious that they are in the process of lovemaking, not pleasure-making.

"Absolute abandonment" is not quite right—if restricted to pleasure; as an opposite, among other opposites, the overall experience of love is most certainly "abandoned to"—so much so that, even in the profound experience of explicit pleasure—which is never without explicit spirit—the unconscious relationship is such that the Third Element, love, cannot help rising. This overall quality, the Third Element, is, as I have said many times before, *the reconciling agent for all opposites*, sexual opposites among them. Proceeding from behind, between and around them, the Third Element, in the guise of love, banishes all hope pleasure might have of usurping the status quo—which it might have if it were minus spirit. Love having bestowed upon spirit *the power to give*, spirit then deputizes for love within even the unconscious depths.

We all have to grow up into the man and woman we actually are. This is the purpose of consciousness, set up specifically to dig out the contents of our hidden unconscious. But do not assume that, within unconsciousness, man and woman were originally a party to explicit pleasure; for, in unity, the opposites were not separated. Pleasure there was, in abundance, but it maintained its unity with spirit—precisely because of its unconsciousness. Nevertheless, *within their unconsciousness*, primitive man and woman *know* the difference; which enabled them to pleasure each other without inhibition—and without shame. Knowing the difference, our primitives have the opportunity, *just like us*, to dismiss love from their awareness, in order all the more to enjoy absolute pleasure.

But, all the time, whether we are aware or unaware, conscious or unconscious, *love is present*; in pleasure, we give and receive; the more fire I can inspire in you, the more fire you inspire in me—to our mutual benefit. Is that not love?

What, then, you may ask, is the difference between sex and illicit sex? The answer is, simply, that illicit sex is not sex; it is not either genuine or innocent sexuality. We know it is not innocent; what makes it ungenuine?

The Sanctity and Profanity of Sexuality

The One Woman

As you expose your lovely pink-tipped young breasts
before me—
Utterly for me—
I know that, within that whitest bosom
Palpitates the heart of hearts.
Everything without your body
Reveals the exquisite world within.
I would paint a picture,
Not just of your manifest exterior,
But also of that yearning Essence
Thrusting its way through the naked contours,
Towards me,
Drawing my evident maleness,
With all the force of its masterly body behind it,
Into your divine reaches;
To slake in one, interminable moment,
The long pent-up needs of a once-shattered heart.
I cannot hide from you, this once,
Whom I mean…
Venus only appears once,
Though there may be a universe of sisters behind her.
Never did I hide, though,
That you were the One Woman above All others—

Concealing, beneath your redolent frame
The Olympian pantheon of goddesses.

*   *   *

The reason lies not so much in the means of expression as in the motives behind it. The motives are: to be as dirty as possible—quite simply—so dirty that it bears no resemblance whatever to sexual behaviour. You may find that strange, considering the way we go at each other!—declaring ourselves as rudely as possible, working each other up into a frenzy of lust!—behaving in just as 'dirty' a way, in fact! *What is the difference?* This is a question which exercises us all. I will settle it.

What we have to realize is that conscious, or civilized, man and woman no longer consist of just a body. Primitive people are completely mindless, not far removed from animals, in fact; we only acquired a psyche when consciousness came in—because, before consciousness, *no-one existed*: "I think, therefore I am". All that could possibly be called existence was held within that *potentially-existing thing* known as the Collective Unconscious; so collective was it—is it—that its only possible means of existence was through *the conscious individual—he, or she, who realizes himself.* In realizing himself, man raises his unconscious potentiality into the light of day, thereby endowing it with life, just as sunlight brings alive a plant on wakening it from its midnight slumbers. The plant, of course, was only temporarily asleep—or non-existent—whereas man has been permanently asleep—or non-existent—since the dawn of Creation. Creation has created nothing, therefore, until now, in the twenty-first century, when man for the first time becomes man. The sole purpose of Creation—existence itself—has never before been realized.

And so, consciousness and unconsciousness now form a partnership to their mutual benefit. Between these two, as usual, we find the answer to everything. The conscious and unconscious minds combine to form the psyche, without which nothing exists—including sex. Without a mind, sex is, by definition, filthy: purely and simply for that reason. Regard the Whore—the woman you supposedly love. Why do you love her? You love a woman for her qualities—no? Without a mind, she has no qualities—how could she have?—beyond a couple of tits and a cunt—(every man's dream.) In point of fact, this leaves her without even a body; while primitive *man* is satisfied with a mere body, conducting his relations with it honourably, what we call 'civilised' man degrades the body to such an extent that nothing in *his* mind exists but the severed articles of the said tits and cunt—oh, and incidentally, the 'bum'.

Knowing, in our unconscious, that our beloved has a mind, though we are busy fucking the daylights out of her, we surface, at the same time as the girl herself, to have a look at each other; this constitutes consciousness, and what we are actually looking *at is the mind—thrust forward, in unmistakable evidence, through the eyes—the window of the soul. Though her eyes may be closed in the midst of her fuck-happy ecstasy, we are nevertheless aware that, within them, lies the girl's essential—and self-respecting—being. And though, too, we may both be doing things which seem distinctly disrespectful, we are doing them out of pure love—blindly, maybe, but nevertheless knowingly.*

Regarding each other's faces, in this periodical return to consciousness, *we see what it is all about: it is about mind itself*—mind containing soul, heart, personality and character, and consisting, in itself, of the very conscious and unconscious awareness between which we are alternating. Thus, the warp-and-woof of the universe.

EXPLICIT LOVE AND PLATONIC SEX

In lieu of explicit pleasure (and explicit spirit) what most people experience is platonic sex. Even if you have intercourse, you may not necessarily be experiencing true sexuality, since pleasure may be minimal—as expressed by the knight-errant and his lady. This so-called 'love-making' isn't love at all; it is a martyrdom to Puritanism—even though Queen Victoria died, miserable, over a hundred years ago.

Platonic sex all hinges around *conscious and unconscious sex, or pleasure.* Unconscious sex is the original state of unity (non-existence), its opposite is the resultant state of conscious awareness (existence). Being aware, "I think, therefore I am".

Explicit pleasure and explicit spirit mean 'real' sex: sex that 'exists'. That is the meaning behind it. 'Conscious love', therefore, is now revealed to be: *love that exists*. Everything follows from that.

Spirit and pleasure can only become conscious if explicit, and vice-versa; likewise, love itself can only become conscious if explicit. So, an end to the Nineteenth Century! And an end to the Twentieth, which wasn't explicit, but downright obscene.

THE NATURE OF THE WHORE

Shamelessness is the essence of her nature; being on the receiving end of love, she does not, consciously, feel obliged to demonstrate anything of a spiritual nature. At this point, the Whore becomes the Bitch—dedicated to pleasure and nothing else—the more indecent, the better. And I love her for her indecency! You randy, wonderful Bitch! And all for love—but let us not interpose that unwelcome idea.

We cannot think of anything too filthy to contribute to our mutual pleasure-making; the identity of the Whore must be preserved. She is not just 'the recipient of pleasure'; she is the *active instigator* of pleasure—no measure is too disgraceful, sex, after all, being an essentially pernicious experience—sado-masochistic, in fact; that well-known, derogatory term being intended to condemn all masturbators. But in fact it doesn't condemn anybody, since sado-masochism in itself is a part of the underlying innocence of sexuality; even in her disgrace, the Whore, or Bitch, is absolutely self-respecting. The attempt to reduce each other to the ultimate exponent of lust, is designed for no less a purpose than to draw us together, through love—lust *being* love. The aim of lust is to reveal to the partners their innermost, ultimate nature; that is love. The idea of fucking, the hell-bent, unstoppable desire to stuff that girl into oblivion, specifically expresses the intention of absolute love itself. "A standing cock ain't got no conscience", and if it had, its vital work would not be done.

Sexual Malefaction

Sexual malefactors are guilty of one thing: <u>putting superficiality first; putting the physical world before reality</u>. The physical, or fleshly, world is totally untrue—having not even one-percent of reality. Cocks and cunts are not the whole body, and, by definition, the parts without the whole are absolutely unreal; <u>the body is reduced to flesh</u>.

The body is naturally innocent, but the flesh is nothing but filthy offal, producing obscene practices in its wake. But, far more than the body, the wrongdoer doesn't know the Mind—the internal, and only, reality; the essence, or mobile spirit. Distinguish, here, between the spirit of the heart, and the spirit which fills, and flows throughout, the body: <u>the spirit of transformation, or Libido, which transforms itself between the spirit of the heart and that of pleasure, while remaining, above all, the spirit of Mind; the Third Element, rising between, enveloping, and coursing within. Three In One, One In Three</u>.

*   *   *

"The gun must go through" at all costs, and this frenetic bucking and heaving saves the day every time; the very absence of conscience ensures that the priceless purposes of sex are carried out under all circumstances and on every occasion. Life itself depends on the ruthless determination of man—even in the perverted instances of rape and illicit sex. Man is only carrying out what he is charged with—what he is given a penis for. If it were not for that, my sweetheart would never be satisfied. A good fucking, therefore, is what we are all after, and God will under no circumstances condemn man for having a randy cock.

Human law may hang a man for rape, and society may ostracize its sexual offenders; but this is not *God's* law; God's law is tempered with love and mercy—and understanding. He welcomes home the sexual offender precisely because he has been condemned by society— the Lord's particular enemy. *God has come to earth to condemn society; there is nothing in society worth saving, or to be commended.* Civilization is rotten to the core, and civilization itself is responsible, by its very laws, for the perversions in its midst.

*   *   *

Whore and Rake temporarily in abeyance, my love and I declare, between ourselves, the most uncompromising devotion; and at the finalizing of this platonic contract, we are inspired to such tenderness for each other that I am at once moved to the expression of violence; tearing her trousers off, I yank her pants right down, showing no mercy, and *leaving her in no doubt that she is bare*. Having no option, as a consequence of her resulting condition, I part her legs roughly and forcefully introduce my very masculine parts into that lovely little place, exposed and waiting for me. Upon that, pleasure being pleasure—not too restrained, we hope, by love—I vigorously effect the business required, and my little sweetheart receives it with the greatest physical delight. Relentlessly I fuck her, forcing the very lights of consciousness out in favour of the charming little bitch's ultimate desire for complete sensual oblivion.

Stoking passion upon passion, by words and the explicit activity of our bodies—our genitals in particular—we drive each other into ever-mounting fever, finally resulting in a blind frenzy—of sheer joy: the perfect amalgam of pleasure and love.

Love having been delivered by its opposite, we subside in the fervently-realised carnal and spiritual fulfilment of all that so-hectic effort—Whore satiated, and Mother in her tender reverie.

Let no-one dare say this was not Love.

*   *   *

That was life itself. Sex is a celebration of life—in the most essential, and vital, form. Those erotic moments are the intense expression of Creation in its white-hot heat. We share this, the most cherished gift from God, to comfort each other in the coldness and darkness of life's long journey of suffering—otherwise unrelieved. It is our *only* comfort, for which your beautiful, and voluptuous, body was given expressly. Physical voluptuousness is to be enjoyed in as explicit a way as possible.

Sex, as we know, is indecent. *It is conducted for the sake of indecency.* Indecency is always irresistible, *and all women desire to be degraded*—purely for the sake of it, too. What could be a greater expression of devotion to your husband than the total submission to his will—*to his wish to annihilate you in one final moment of lust and love combined?—the love to give it, and the physical, wanton lust to carry it out.* If I had not the desire to fuck you into Kingdom Come, with all the glorious indecency at my disposal, the purposes of love would never be carried out. For love is to be loved; you are *to be loved*; and I am *to love you.* How could love accomplish itself other than by addressing the innermost need of man and woman: to be absolutely overwhelmed by pulsating pleasure in its rawest, most acute form?

Pleasure and Love

The purpose of love is pleasure, the purpose of pleasure is love. But, finally, there is only love; in love, through pleasure.

* * *

The Whore is not a loveless bitch; she is the most honourable servant of pleasure, and only becomes rampant when divorced from love—to which she is, by nature, affianced. The common conception of this much-maligned heroine is erroneously derived from the depraved representatives of civilization's perverted behaviour.

* * *

Can you not understand this inviolable truth: that sex is love—and nothing else?

* * *

"Pleasure is love, and love pleasure". "Love is the only thing that ennobles it"; *but what love ennobles has to be there in the first place.* Love cannot ennoble pleasure unless it is indecent; what excuse would love have for exerting its influence as the Mother, if she had not a fractious daughter to contend with? Daughters are fractious; they need pleasure, and they always kick over the traces to get it. Pleasure would hold no attraction for them *if the Mother was seen to sanction it; the Mother has to be rebelled against.*

It is not pleasure which is indecent; the indecency is purely the desire of the daughter to fly in the face of her Mother's demands. She has to do this; she has to rebel; *she has to feel naughty.*

Take away naughtiness and you deprive the daughter of the primary quality of her life. Sex is an expression of naughtiness; sex is a *celebration* of naughtiness.

We have the Mother—goodness; we have the Whore—badness; the indispensable relationship of good and evil: life itself.

THE SANCTITY OF EVIL

Why did God, apparently knowingly, introduce such evil propensities into the world? Let me say at once that 'evil', in the following context, is not the same as 'wickedness'.

Casanova's beloved whore—so many of them—cried out in sheer ecstasy, as he fucked her into the knowledge that she was evil; she knew, she experienced, her own evil nature. And she worshipped Casanova for showing it to her—for giving it to her in that glorious, frantic fuck. With her own, exuding spunk, mingled with his, in their mutually-engaged, infamous genitals, they deliberately raised each other to a frenzy of lust. This is life, this is evil, this is love.

Love, at the back of it all, determines that we should feel evil—*determines the way in which we feel evil*; love, herself, bestows evil upon us—to be enjoyed with every tumultuous fuck we can muster. Enjoy evil!

Evil has to be enjoyed to produce a fuck, and a fuck has to be produced to express your love for your woman. The more you love your woman, the more evil you give her—the more you make her *feel* evil. She has to feel evil because she is a whore, and whores like to feel evil. Whores are, in fact, the *personification* of evil, uncontrollable in pursuit of their own nature; for they have to know they are evil—otherwise they will never know *who they are*: "I am evil, therefore I am; I am, therefore I am evil".

God put men and women on earth to be evil. Does it not say in the bible that man is evil?—that his very nature is irrevocable evil? Let it remain so, Man *is* evil because *he has to be* evil—in order to enjoy himself; if we are not put on earth to enjoy ourselves, what the hell are we put on earth for? We are not here to give alms to those who can't enjoy themselves; because, if the rest of us can't enjoy ourselves either, who the hell *is* going to enjoy himself? God's last words to man, as he places him in his mother's womb, as a little child waiting to be born, are, "Son, enjoy yourself at all costs, because life is so miserable that you'll get fuck all apart from a good fuck! So, therefore, I've given you a cock to facilitate your fucking; do not dishonour it by using it for anything else. If the Archbishop tells you it is only to be used on Sundays— in the sanctity of the church, where only the nuns are likely to get hold of it—don't believe him! You won't get any pleasure whatever! How can a nun dedicated to the overthrow of evil, give you the very pleasure that evil is put on earth for? I swear to you, my lad, that I have given you a cock to enjoy and a beautiful young girl, on the end of it, to help you enjoy it; how are either you, or she, going to give yourselves any pleasure if there is no substance in it? How can a nun's hand inspire any joy in your cock if she wields it without any meaning? How can a man enjoy the attentions of his lady-love *if she is determined not to give him any pleasure?*

Selfishness

No selfishness is permitted,
For selfishness brings ugliness;
Those youngsters, those teenage louts,
Would do well to keep
Their cocks in their hands,
Until they have grown up
And mastered themselves.

*   *   *

The whole thing revolves around Paradox. Know thyself—know thou art being fucked—or thou art doing the fucking. Without self-knowledge—or the knowledge of good and evil—you will never know yourself, or the *evil that rests within you*. We cannot know ourselves by only knowing the good. *Ninety-nine per cent of each man and woman is evil; only one per cent of us consists of the façade of good which is civilization.* Under that façade is the reality of natural, or instinctive, man and woman. Nature may be innocent—unaware of either good or evil—*but evil pervades the whole of the unconscious mind*—and here, I am distinguishing between Nature and the Unconscious. They have a lot in common—in fact, in many ways they are identical—but, as far as the question of good and evil is concerned, they are diametrically opposed. It is impossible for the notion of good and evil to exist in Nature—the home of Adam and Eve—for Nature is essentially without thought; the notion exists only in the realm of ideas—or consciousness. Nature is undoubtedly unconscious, but she is not synonymous with the unconscious mind itself. The unconscious mind is independent of Nature, leaving us with the inescapable conclusion that it exists very much nearer the surface of man's psyche—*directly under it, in fact. Actually, where is the unconscious mind?* Is it in heaven, or is it in hell?— Got it in one; I have proved elsewhere that heaven is the abode of consciousness, and that earth—by all accounts, hell—is the abode of unconsciousness; if you like it better, God—the chief incumbent of heaven—is consciousness i.e. the Supra-Conscious itself, and man—the chief resident on earth—is so abysmally stupid that he is *unconsciousness* itself. We are not dealing with physical locations but with the parameters of mind.

Enter, the Subconscious:-

Evil is *conscious knowledge*. Subtract consciousness and you no longer have evil; when Eve ate the apple, she was at once visited by the consciousness of Good and Evil. But the transactions between Good and its opposite can only be possible through the mediating factor of the subconscious margin between consciousness and unconsciousness. So subtle and complex, and paradoxical, is this area that it has become the focal point of the conscious and unconscious minds and, consequently, of human relationships.

As far as the sanctity, or evil, of such relationships is concerned, we need only regard the first section of my essay "The Naked Savage Holds the Secret"; we see there the essential idea of transition between the two conceptions, to and from the modes of conscious and unconscious awareness.

Man's own evil is what will save him. Evil is good—while still remaining evil.

Love is the place of evil—the one and only place— the saving place.

To save themselves, every woman must become a

woman and every man a man. Gone will be Florence Nightingale, and gone will be the gentleman. A woman cannot be pleasured by a gentleman: she needs to know her own evil; and then her gratitude will know no bounds.

Released into her own evil, by a knowledgeable man, woman will become the whore she always was by nature, and the purposes of Love will be served.

Know thy own evil.

Casanova was a man—and all his women knew him to be so. And he put it about, he did—with that long, raking penis of his, that every woman in Venice worshipped. For it gave them such incredible pleasure: the sheer delight of knowing and experiencing their evil. They knew their own nature; their ultimate reality—their humility—before God. And their glory.

God made them so—to know their evil. Evil was put in no other place than Love; evil in any other place is good.

*   *   *

I am not speaking of 'wickedness'; wickedness is not only dark, like evil, *but also ugly*—ugly, un-self-respecting, and without grace. For our beloved evil is nothing if not beautiful. Look at those roguish, lovely eyes! *They* do not bespeak ugliness; a loaded challenge, maybe, but a challenge, ultimately, to the *Beauty* between us. Satiated flesh has the Beauty of *meaning*, if not the Beauty of *appearance*. And the sanctity of evil resides in its innocence, even if it *is* a hard-played game.

* * *

The purpose of civilization is to convert our unconscious lusts and desires into individual form; in directing an unconscious mass of collective instinct into the very narrow receptacle of the individual's brain, the aim of evolution is achieved; the original state of Unity—unconsciousness—must be ended, because only when man becomes conscious of himself will he begin to live, for the first time: "I am conscious, therefore I am".

* * *

The woman's heartfelt cry expresses a profound and ecstatic immersion in consummate evil, with complete mental and physical satisfaction. The major satisfaction probably took place mentally rather than physically, mental wickedness (rather, evil) as we all know, taking the overwhelmingly superior role over its physical counterpart. Both experiences add up to the most incredible psychological crescendo in the relations of man and woman. Not a single human being has ever been conscious of it, and most people have not even experienced it.

Casanova's major contribution was to present the reality of sex, and to put it around two or three hundred women in Venice (or wherever). These satisfied customers are probably the only recipients of genuine sexuality in the Western world, since the art of love was lost, apart from a few isolated pockets of resistance. The French are not bad at it, the Argentineans are quite good at it—when they are not preoccupied with brothels—and the Poles are particularly good at it…

Rani

A girl glimpsed on a train. Showing some pimples, and great distress, she had obviously been betrayed—'seduced', in the real meaning of the word—by her boyfriend.

Giving herself to him with all the love only a girl like her knows, she has been led into ways that would make your blood curdle—entirely against her will and her dismayed self-respect. Despite herself, she is now sold to lust; once having tasted irresistible Orgasm, she, like many another generous young woman is now eaten alive by the fires of illicit concupiscence: this beautiful, noble young thing, through no fault of her own, has been damned by the treacheries of Sex.

I could have saved her: I loved her—though at a moment's glance. But, unfortunately, I am not in a position to move even against lust; and even though I may love a woman madly, I cannot abandon my life-long commitment to chastity—until the One Woman releases me.

But my passion for Rani has taught me one thing; that the Phallus is not a symbol of sex—but rather, that sex is a symbol of the Phallus. The Phallic symbol denotes the masculine principle—the erect position of the male psychological attitude as against the supine position of the female attitude; in other words, Consciousness against Instinct.

So Rani, in her unwilling infamy—by her sacrifice—has inspired the Son of God. When she returns to heaven, she will be remembered—whatever happens to her on earth.

I could kill myself for abandoning her.

*   *   *

Most of the remainder are divided between platonic sex, on the one hand, and illicit sex on the other. In the one case, neither love nor pleasure exists, and in the other, only pleasure exists.

* * *

Sigmund Freud himself tried to save the show by subtracting Florence Nightingale altogether; but this led to the unfortunate result that love disappeared from sex forever. So now we all go around shagging like rabbits, with no restraint; admittedly we don't wish for restraint, because the essence of shagging is in its total abandonment, but we do have to realize that enough is enough, and a line has to be drawn somewhere.

That somewhere is spirit; and though spirit does not wish to impose restraint, by its very presence it ensures that *pleasure is given, not just received*. The restraining influence comes from the gesture of giving; and by giving, paradoxically, you will be determined to go out of your way to *lose* all restraint for the sake of your lady-love.

* * *

Shittiness pervades the whole body, and is not restricted to the genitals or to any other part. A girl's loveliness does indeed contain her propensity for, her desire for, this pernicious element. It brings a bloom to her cheeks.

As a puking and mulling infant shits his nappies liberally, and grows into a strapping lad, so a young woman lays the groundwork of her lovemaking, forking manure over her lower regions, to grow strongly into the upper reaches of Beauty untold.

Beauty rules all. Her face—the exquisitely flushed and blooming head of the rose—is the edifice of the body, *the focus*.

Above all, the eyes.
Always the eyes,
Always the face
—never the body,
That thorny and treacherous stem;
However beautiful it is,
It always palls before the apertures of the soul,
Without which it will lead the most experienced lover astray.

The garden depends on fertilizer, from the bowels of animals, and even humans; and from it springs life, in all its vital glory. Let not that area of genital foliage, symbolizing, as it does, the very fountain of Life, go unacknowledged; for, then, truly, would God's bequest go spurned. Death would return to the earth, after your Saviour's sacrifice in bringing Truth, Love and sexual explicitness to all you young men and maidens, unspoiled by iniquity, who hold the happiness of humankind within your unawoken loins.

Herein lies the resolution of age-old Good-and-Evil: resolved within man's own shit—the common-ground, the breeding-ground; font of all wisdom, source of all Beauty. The illicit whore is saved by the Natural Whore, *the Natural Whore is saved by the illicit whore; evil is saved by evil, evil becomes good.*

The naked challenge of a lovely girl is something to die for: naked fire, the fire of both the anal and genital regions, completely consuming in its rapture, rising throughout body and soul, and gladdening those bewitching, adoring eyes. Within those apertures resides the evidence of Absolute Good, where good and evil are reconciled, spirit and pleasure performing their essential service as opposites.

*   *   *

THE INTEGRITY OF THE WHORE

Perversion comes about, invariably, as the result of exaggeration and dissociation: the exaggerated and dissociated expression of something once perfectly innocent and normal. Sado-Masochism, and every other perversion, was originally a perfectly viable sexual procedure.

All lapses from orthodoxy proceed ultimately from the surrender of self-respect—thus determining the occurrence of exaggeration-dissociation—self-respect itself being the regulatory mechanism put in place to ensure the survival of personal integrity—without which *there is no person*. The disintegration of the person, or self—in other words, its 'dis-integrity'—probably originates *from the basic dissociation of opposites—and consequently from their exaggeration also*. The chief pair of opposites involved in this dissociation *are the fundamental conscious and unconscious functions*—from which everything follows.

Self-respect is usually withdrawn from oneself by oneself—almost by will. No-one else, and no outside agency, can do it. It is, in fact, not 'almost by will', but quite definitely by will. The self loses its respect for itself *when the consciousness of self vanishes*. Self-consciousness has nothing to do with teenage embarrassment; *consciousness of self is one thing only: Ego*. Egoic consciousness is the area, or location, of the function of consciousness itself—directed, by the self, both internally into the mind, and externally towards the outside world.

Egoic consciousness, therefore, is obviously vitally important; *and when it is withdrawn, we equally obviously become blind—blind to ourselves and blind to the world. Self-respect vanishes when egoic consciousness vanishes.* [the 'ego', according to its Latin derivation, means, simply, 'I'; and 'I' am conscious of two things: myself (self-consciousness) and the outside world (consciousness of other than myself).

Self-respect is never, in fact, destroyed; *it merely vanishes into unconsciousness*, in which it lingers, maybe indefinitely, while occasionally prompting an acknowledgement of its presence in the consciousness remaining above it; these 'pricks of conscience' may or may not be sufficient to persuade the conscious mind to take note of them, and thereby to acknowledge the existence of their source: the much abused self—from which all conscious recognition, i.e. self-respect, has been retracted.

God Is Absolute Consciousness

The question of the Hermaphrodite nature of God (as raised in the 'One And The Many') is answered in the fact that what we are dealing with is not the difference between, or combination of male and female, or man and woman, <u>but between masculine and feminine. In God, both masculinity and femininity exist in equal measure, in contrast to his exclusively male 'identity'. God is, essentially, consciousness—the male principle.</u>

Why, you may ask, is God not, in equal measure, female (as opposed to feminine)? God is not in any way unconscious, the female (or feminine) principle. Nevertheless, both the feminine principle and the female principle represent unconsciousness; is God, therefore, equally conscious and unconscious, in contrast to our claim that he is essentially conscious? I say he is <u>essentially</u> conscious—not <u>exclusively</u> so—meaning that, though he undoubtedly possesses unconsciousness, its obverse is actually the major factor. The impasse contained in these statements is resolved in the distinction between the male and female principles and a particular man and woman. Although God, as a particular man, is conscious, his identity as a man is over and above his male, or conscious, <u>character</u>; his actual being remains above his mere characterization.

God, as I have said before, is 'Absolute Consciousness'; that does not mean he is <u>exclusively</u> conscious, but absolute consciousness is identical to the 'Supra-Conscious', which, as we know, is a combination of conscious and unconscious, meaning that absolute consciousness itself possesses unconsciousness. The obvious implication in the term 'Supra-Conscious' is that, somehow, absolute consciousness, while being a product of both conscious and unconscious, <u>is actually above both</u>. The Third Element, in this instance, reserves for itself the quality of consciousness above unconsciousness, thus transforming the hybrid nature of the ultimate, or absolute, consciousness into a single, and very different, identity. While still retaining the character of consciousness, God's defining quality is therefore raised to a level which surpasses that; but, while taking on an entirely different and higher significance, it yet remains a combination of its two individual parts: <u>three in one, one in three—the Holy Trinity</u>.

The Holy Trinity, as we know, is a synonym for the Godhead, which consists of God the Father, God the Son, and God the Holy Ghost—the Holy Ghost being, essentially, consciousness, or the Supra-Conscious—common to both the Father and the Son, <u>and mediating itself between them. Three in One, One in Three.</u>

*   *   *

These facts are the ultimate mystery, the ultimate truth, towards which man's philosophical and religious quest has always been directed.

*   *   *

Integrity, self-respect, shame, guilt, conscience and inhibition—all the same thing—vanish at the drop of a hat on meeting the predations of psychiatry, which never fail to persuade the average punter that sex is for pleasure, and should be indulged in as often, and as dirtily, as possible. So powerful is the ability of psychiatrists to persuade, and so weak is the ability of the average man to resist, that the self-respect of the whole Western world has capitulated at a stroke. So we have prostitutes, in ever-greater numbers, getting their fannies off day and night in the brothel, schoolgirls getting their fannies off day and night, except when having lessons, in the back of a car, the average housewife reserving *her* fanny for the inglorious arrival of her husband back from work—and all the dirtier for it—and Sally and Fanny getting *their* smelly varieties off behind the idiot-board on the television. This is the Whore, indeed!

This is not the Whore I know and love; this is the illicit whore, with a fanny as big and smelly as her lack of self-respect can possibly make it. My Whore loves—even if, much of the time, unconsciously—and though she is concerned to excite her man as much as possible, with all her woman's alluring ways, she possesses this one quality: the dignity of personal integrity. She never loses it; she never surrenders the one quality which unites her, and should unite all women, with the Lord—her sexual master.

*   *   *

Self-respect received its prototype withdrawal when consciousness visited the original state of unity, in which the opposites were unseparated. When the opposites became separated, as the direct result of the visit from consciousness, the element of self-respect suddenly vanished from the face of the earth. Gone was God; gone was beauty, gone was love. Instead was left the raging Whore—the illicit Whore—Godless, masterless, and uncontrollable. *Uncontrollable because pleasure had become explicit—and divorced from spirit.* Normally, however, the mere fact that the opposites have become separated would not warrant dismay or the automatic dissolution of integrity, because the relationship between them would still be preserved; but our innocent bitch, our charming little wanton, says goodbye to the mother and betakes herself, pants wet and spunk flowing, to the brothel, where she climbs aboard the bed and salutes every man in town with her legs in the air. Legs in the air or not, her integrity has most certainly disintegrated; dismembered both physically and mentally, she presents her army of paramours with a bum, a pair of tits (if you're lucky) and that thing in the middle which could no longer be called a place of love. In fact, love is so absent that there is not any glue to hold together the straying parts, or opposites. With the penetration of unity, or unconsciousness, by that cold-blooded, conscious outsider, the cohesion of Innocence is lost, and Pandora's box is exposed to the world with its multifarious, unrelated contents.

But Pandora's Box contains the potential solution. *Herein is contained Creation's Paradox.* Within Paradox itself we find the meaning of all; it is not a bald concept; it breathes, it farts, it stinks—it is Life, both varnished and unvarnished. And it furnishes us with the resolution of all our conflicts; presented to us two thousand years ago for the first time, in the symbol of the Cross, its extended arms represent the dichotomy of all opposites, *and at the same time their reconciliation.* That is the wonder of the Cross—its meaning. Wood for the murder of his body, symbol for the suffocation of his mind.

The contents of Pandora's Box are authorized by Christ's crucifixion to act as the building blocks for Creation's purpose; which is, to assault all peace and tranquillity—that is to say, harmony—with the very intention of building it up again; so, life and death, love and lust, instinct and consciousness—all designed to fight in the Battle for Life; thereupon to be converted into the very thing that *saves* Life. Harmonious Unity is broken up into Pandora's thousand pieces: death, disintegration—*the extinction of self-awareness, or self-*

respect. Self-respect is founded on wholeness, or integration—integrity. Consequently, if the cohesion of the self is assaulted, its respect for itself vanishes into the dissolution of its many parts: spirit drifts apart from pleasure, femininity from masculinity, tits from bums, and, finally, consciousness from unconsciousness. We are left in total disarray; everyone goes around shagging everyone else, and a right merry time is had by all! Freud is the ring-master, and Darwin is the master of ceremonies. In Sweden, 'free-love' is declared; this does not mean you are not obliged to pay for it, but simply that there is no love involved in the first place: if everyone shags everyone else, without distinction, and without even paying for it, either with a five-pound note or half-a-pound of butter (which might at least do as a lubricant for her over-indulgent fanny) you have automatically subtracted the very purpose for which love, or sex, was intended: individuality. The only thing which distinguishes us, or used to, from copulating dogs, is the difference, and, therefore, resulting union, between us; with no distinction between one whore and another, how do I know who I am shagging? I do require some identification, otherwise I might find myself shagging my own Mother, which, apparently, is acceptable in Sweden under the 'right to free access' law granted to all and sundry, the 'Rights of Man' entitling us to do whatever we like whenever we like—free of charge. So there is 'free love', after all!

Having, then, extinguished all semblance of individuality, Sweden is a collective knocking-shop, noted for its incredible immaturity, throughout the international community, and for the even more incredible stupidity which brought this about in the first place. Doctored by Freud, and also seduced by Women's Lib's determination to eliminate femininity, Swedish society is now minus the men to do the shagging and the women to be shagged, since femininity is the only thing that distinguishes women from men and men from women. Furthermore, femininity is the very thing that enables both men and women to love. But then, you don't want love, do you? The whole idea of 'free love' is actually to do away with love altogether, since it always proves a hindrance; after all, if you are intending to implant as many illegitimate babies as possible, being the overwhelmingly loving man you are, what good is it if every woman closes her legs on the grounds that she is married? You see, although marriage may have received the thumbs-down from Sigmund Freud, it is actually the mainstay of society, and, indeed, of individuality—which is its very purpose, both men and women needing the sanctuary of private communion to develop their mutual needs in this regard. It's not much good, is it, if the opportunity to realize your purpose on earth—the very aim of evolution—is suddenly withdrawn on the edict of an Austrian witch-doctor?

The unbelievable ignorance of society's pillars is determined by their total lack of thought. Individuality is brought about by thinking; thinking is brought about by individuality; but neither of them lives in a vacuum: *they need love to nourish them. Individuality demands a unique home, run by a unique housewife.* The substitution of a 'partnership'—an idea so dear to today's punters— for the sanctity of love, speaks volumes: no, you cannot love in a 'partnership'—'partners in crime', perhaps? Even more appalling than the idea produced by it, is the experience of loveless sex; in 'free love', love is actually extracted in favour of a nameless, mindless *non-existence*. This is in fact the intention, whether or not it is conscious.

Non-existence consists of the absence of self-consciousness, or self-respect—two fundamental qualities in individuality. Consequently, without its two mainstays, individuality itself vanishes, leaving a total void—a void that stinks in the face of God. But, of course, God doesn't exist...

The experience of loveless sex is one of promiscuity (even within marriage). Apparently, the more you put your love about, the more generous you are, and the greater the number of females who receive your undoubted abilities; the trouble is that the only benefit those females end up with is venereal disease.

The sheer immaturity, again, and utter stupidity of modern men and women is quintessentially represented in the idea of 'partnership': the daftness that produced this proposition runs so deep in modern public, and private, affairs that there is very little hope—indeed none at all—of eradicating it. Daftness will remain; daftness is the defining feature of human psychology—leading directly to the abandonment of thought, and to the ludicrous conclusion that love can be conducted on the basis of an 'open relationship',—where one's options are so 'open' that one is granted permission, from the very start, to abandon one's partner at the drop of a hat, and take up a better proposition elsewhere. Love is gone, because love was never there.

The heart is where pleasure takes place. Midway between head and body, or mind and pleasure, the heart distils all Passion; Passion *belongs* to the heart, being the Third Element in which are united the opposites of Mother and Whore (conscious and unconscious). Under pleasure thrives the meaning and purpose of it: *giving and receiving*: in a word, Love. However unconscious we may be, in the midst of our determination to enjoy, *we know why we are doing it, and what we are doing.* The woman in front of me, desperate in her throes of ecstasy, *is ever the loving angel administering our mutual pleasure*. Disguising it from herself, the more to enjoy this experience, she maintains a watchful eye over propriety.

Passion, furthermore, unites conscious with unconscious, urging us to emerge and re-submerge from the one into the other. And, in the end, the purpose of lovemaking is revealed in the Supra-Consciousness that results from their union.

It is actually thought clever and sophisticated to spurn love for pleasure—to demonstrate your cowardly fear of society's displeasure by deliberately destroying your birthright. Your mates, themselves a set of cowardly poltroons, take Women's Lib's high-flown edicts as an excuse for dishing the dirt on an imaginary grievance against their long-suffering parents. Being told, by Freud again, that parents, mothers, love, and God are 'not necessary', they turn against their own family, emotionally if not physically, and reject all the decency hitherto lavished on them.

The immediate policy *is to declare yourself against the very society you do cowardly obey*. So, a curmudgeon, a double curmudgeon. Being too craven to come out against your mates, you nevertheless assume the mantle of 'heroism' and announce to your parents: "I am going to have as many illegitimate babies as I possibly can; I am going to degrade myself with men every night; and I most certainly am not going to get married. All because you are totally inoffensive, and because I wish to assert my falsely-assumed identity".

This is what society demands that you do. Oh no, not obviously. And your pusillanimity persuades you to take up your egotistic instincts and attack, with all the fury of a weakling, the very hand that feeds you. Thus, society itself revealed: founded, quintessentially, on cowardice. Not a man escapes.

Love requires commitment; how can you love someone if you are not committed to them? And how can you be committed if you are not prepared to marry them to indicate it? Marriage carries conviction: the declaration that you love them unreservedly.

Apparently, the idea behind a partnership is that you are keeping your options open: in telling a man that you are not going to marry him, you are in fact saying, "I don't like you well enough to stay with you; in fact, at the first (or second) opportunity, I shall probably take myself off with another poor sucker. And if we have those children you offered me, I don't care sufficiently about them to give them security: let them run about in a constant state of consternation, wondering if they've got any parents".

The crass stupidity and infernality in all this, beggars belief. How could anyone be so unaware of the significance of their actions? (That is not a compliment).

There is no such thing as sex.

*   *   *

Divine Love I

The Most Vital Point in the Christian Religion

Dear X

I am going to ask you to be very understanding, and to bring all your womanly intuition, plus your compassion, to bear. What I have to discuss is, on the face of it, of the utmost indecency, being God's revelation of his own sexuality; I hope you don't stop reading because of it, though I wouldn't blame you if you did. But you must keep reading, out of what little regard you have left for me, because my future depends on it, *yours, too, and, indeed, the fate of the whole Christian religion.*

I, as the representative of the Christian religion, have, as perhaps my chief concern, the proposition to the world that, "it should not judge by appearances". A well-known maxim, and not likely to excite much interest, except that, viewed in the light of what 1 have to say, it will be seen to be of the utmost significance. Such significance has it that evolution, and the future of mankind, depend on it. This point may prove to be my real crucifixion, because if no-one believes me, Christ is really damned; and the most damning thing of all would be if you did not believe me—my own sweetheart—or you were until last week, when this whole business blew up in your face. A more appalling thing, in fact, never faced Christendom.

Fortunately, after sixty years of having everything thrown at me, this latest acquisition only in fact serves to increase my self-belief—which it was intended to do. However incredible it may seem, this very cataclysmic debacle was set up, among many others of a minor variety, in order to produce the final evidence of my identity, upon which ultimately depends my release from the physical death forming my crucifixion. Finally realising my identity, furthermore, which is obviously a mental preoccupation, I will be enabled to release myself, also, *psychologically*. The significance is that the *combination* of the physical and mental factors adds up to my overall *psychological crucifixion*.

Those of you who have been following my various writings, should be aware of the huge importance that psychology has for the future development of humanity, and therefore you must also be aware of the inestimable importance of the emergence of a *totally new psychological symbol*: the psychological crucifixion of Christ. We have moved from the basically physical awareness of man, as he was two thousand years ago—symbolized by a wooden, therefore physical, cross—to the threshold of the truly psychological age.

The relation of the physical and mental worlds—psychology—is therefore presented in a new light. We have first to take on board the fact that physical 'reality' is actually a total illusion; that surface appearances, however solid, merely disguise their underlying nature of 'flux'; that is to say, their constantly-moving interior, whether this consists of colliding atoms or a gurgling stomach. Apply a microscope to any object, presumed to be dead because of its outward disguise, and you will see the teeming millions of atoms and molecules, very much alive. Life, you see, consists of exactly that: 'eternal flux', in which all atoms and molecules are engaged in what could be called 'perpetual motion'. Motion being the most obvious distinction between life and death—after all, a 'dead body' doesn't move of its own volition, not being possessed of a will, or soul, the usual criteria of the living state—we should be aware at once that all physical objects in which motion appears, are, by that very fact, alive. Their motion is indeed determined by a will—the Universal Will, which drives all matter, from the upper-echelon of plants to the lower level of stones and other such things.

It is necessary to prove the existence of the Universal

Will, which belongs, of course, to the Universal Mind. Science has never admitted the existence of the Universal Mind, because of the incredibly simple fact that it can't see it. Nothing exists, according to science, if you can't see it; visibility furnishes proof. The average scientist wouldn't acknowledge his omission in this regard, *because he couldn't see that, either*; it has no physical presence. Even an idea has no existence, apparently, because you can't see it; existence has to be physical, therefore visible. The average scientist, again, would not claim that an idea did not exist, because that would be crass; but that is the underlying assumption. Science would actually agree with the finding of esoteric thinkers, that *everything is material, or physical*. But that just shows how stupid both science and esoteric thought can be. Of course everything is material!—why shouldn't it be? *But everything is also spiritual, or mental.* The incredibly stupid resolution that everything is exclusively physical, issues from the further shortcoming of science in being utterly unable to think. If science adopted the time-honoured custom of thinking, it would immediately see that, quite obviously, "There are more things in heaven, or on earth, than meet the eye"; but it doesn't think, and consequently it turns things over to unconscious assumptions, with the result that the most egregious statements issue forth without ever being reconciled with reality.

The undoubted fact that both physical and mental reality is present in the world does not dissuade our 'intellectuals' from arguing about it, and the more they argue, the deeper they get stuck in the mire. For years this argument has raged back and forth, without getting anywhere, in a magazine called *The Journal of Consciousness Studies*—run by a fellow called Anthony Freeman. Observing this condition of impasse, I, as is my wont, offered the perfectly obvious solution—several times—but I was totally ignored, and never achieved publication, due primarily to Freeman's woeful lack of intellectual ability—he is, basically, a scientist, and should never have been put in charge of a magazine for thinkers. He had the cheek to tell me that my paper was not sufficiently original to be published, and that it did not furnish a solution anyway—both these statements issuing, evidently, from a mind too inadequate to assess the truth, which centred around the factor of Paradox— the only basis on which to address the problem, and without which there is no solution. It is this factor of Paradox that has prevented everyone, by way of their abysmal lack of intelligence, from understanding the problem, and thereby solving it. The first sign of intelligence is the ability to understand paradox, and the absence of that quality is responsible for the almost total failure of Western philosophy in general. Apart from

Kant, Hegel, Schopenhauer, and possibly Nietche (who appears to have been so dumb that he denied the existence of God—if it wasn't he, it was someone else) there has been no-one able to offer a decent theory. Stretching way back to Plato, Aristotle and Socrates, the last people with any pretensions to philosophy, all we have been presented with is vast tomes, with no comprehensive theory at all, dedicated to the minute examination of 'monads' and, further forward in time, to the more extensive elucidation of 'indeterminism'. On reading the investigation into monads, we have to conclude, if we can overcome our boredom, that the author was either shortsighted, or he was simply unable to raise his intellect to a meaningful and significant level. If he was using his 'monads' as particularities, in order to work up a theory involving universals, that would have some point, but he would need to exhibit some consciousness of what he was doing; that, he was singularly lacking, and consequently we didn't get much of a theory out of him at all, but merely a series of half-baked observations. Also blinkered in this regard, for much the same reasons, was the 'philosopher' who concerned himself with indeterminism. He also was a bore, and the first requirement of a philosopher is that you should be interesting. When you concern yourself with indeterminism, or for that matter determinism, you must be aware of the necessity for tipping a wink towards its opposite, *otherwise you deprive yourself of paradox*. It is not enough to pay lip-service to the opposite; you have to embrace it. Otherwise you don't get paradox, and hence no consciousness; paradox breeds consciousness, and consciousness breeds paradox.

Lacking both consciousness and paradox, Western philosophy has continued to bore the pants off us since Socrates snuffed it, and has been so preoccupied with minutiae that I have often been tempted to go in unto them myself and offer the poor buggars a microscope...

The Vicar's Daughter

She fluttered her eyelashes at me in the most becoming fashion, displaying her exquisite nature. But I wasn't having any of that: depriving her of her nether garments (as usual) I at once banished all thoughts of the vicar's daughter, and the two of us, partners in crime, now, proceeded with enthusiasm to dishonour the tradition of decorum.

But, having initially introduced her into a most unusual position, even by my standards, I eventually succeeded in convincing her that she was Joan of Arc and Marilyn Munroe combined; and in this hybrid state she returned to her father's care quite unaware that she had been seduced, being persuaded—quite rightly—that her natural virtue had remained intact. And so, one more charming girl retires from me, satisfied on both counts as Mother and Whore.

*   *   *

The vast majority of modern 'thinkers' have no right to consider themselves philosophers—though there are hordes of them around every pulpit—and, in the case of most of them, they have reached no further distinction than an appointment to the 'resident thinker' on the local council. So many are there of these failed intellectuals that I see them, every day, queuing up at the labour exchange; a most oversubscribed industry. There is only one 'philosopher' per century (and in the last century, it was Jung).

*   *   *

To cut a long story short—particularly as I can't remember what I was saying—I will need to ignore a lot of what I have said above, and launch in from a new angle. I will attempt to prove, from this new point of view, that the universe does indeed possess a mind, and that it actually consists of this mind.

Take the Collective Unconscious—a concept from Carl Jung, my favourite prophet, and the greatest mind in history, next to me. He proceeded me onto earth for the precise purpose of establishing this concept ahead of me, preparing the ground for my exposition. It has always been fashionable to deny Jung's concept—one good fashion deserves another—and do you know why?

Precisely because its meaning is so obvious, precisely because everyone knows the truth of it. No-one before Jung did know the truth, but when this news burst upon the world, *everyone knew at once that this was brimming beneath their awareness: the antidote to consciousness.* That which consciousness had suppressed since the beginning of civilization, was now biting us on the arse. Which is why science at once denied it. Science is founded on the belief that the only thing in existence is physical reality, that there is nothing, furthermore *beneath the surface of physical appearance.* So, therefore, when Jung revealed that there was, science took a back seat. The scientific ego was shattered. And, as ever, ego asserted itself by denying every truth that came against it...

The Living-Death

The Living-Death which Christ endures on the Cross, perhaps to perpetuity, enables the Cosmos, or Creation, to <u>relate</u> the conscious function to the unconscious function, so healing the age-old Schism between the two.

*　　*　　*

Doubly blinded, then, by their belief that visibility is the only truth, and by the ego which prevents them seeing the real truth, scientists continue in their sweet, unconscious way, lording it over the rest of us as the guardians of the physical status quo, and denying us the right to look further.

Having established, on the assumption that you are amenable to logic, and, even further, that you allow yourself access to your unconscious instincts, that the Collective Unconscious does exist, what, we might ask ourselves, does it actually consist of? I don't think anyone would doubt that it resides in the unconscious mind; what is 'collective' about it? We have the Personal (or individual) Unconscious—a well-known and accepted term—with which to contrast it. Both the Collective, and Personal Unconscious probably originating with Jung, you might be expected to accept the one on the basis of the other, since I put it to you that, in this world, we have a fundamental antimony between *individual* reality and *universal* reality; the 'universal' traditionally contrasts with the 'particular'—being philosophically established. So, substituting the term 'individual' for 'particular', and the term 'collective' for 'universal'—these terms being identical in meaning—we can conclude that in both the conscious world of thinking and the unconscious world of instinct, the same basic antimony applies.

On this basis, therefore, let me illustrate the relation of the physical and mental worlds. Taking the mental world to consist of the universal half, we are left with the physical world as the particular half. It is a fact that the universal *penetrates* every aspect of the world, while the particular is *penetrated*. The particular, in essence, is one *part*; the universal, overwhelmingly, *is the whole*. (To take each particular part and describe it as a member of many parts, or indeed the whole, would be to *equate* it with the whole—to identify it. "The whole is more than the sum of its parts"; the particular is the *one* particular part. Use thy imagination).

Having established that the universal is co-incidental with the collective, by association we can see that both the universal and collective are co-incidental with the Whole. If this Whole proves to have the attributes of a mind, we thereby prove that the Universe itself consists of a mind. We have also established that the Collective Unconscious resides behind the façade of physical existence, meaning that the Whole or 'universal' also resides behind physical existence, and, as the Collective Unconscious is acknowledged to be a mind, the Whole, or Universe itself, is proved to be a mind, also.

As far as the 'conscious world of thinking' is concerned, and the 'unconscious world of instinct', the latter provides for the Collective Unconscious, the former accounts for the Individual Conscious. The two together create the Cosmic Consciousness—affiliated to the Cosmic Mind. (According to Jung, the Supra-Conscious, or Cosmic Consciousness, consists of an amalgam of consciousness and unconsciousness.)

UNIVERSAL AND PARTICULAR

The 'universal-particular' principle is upheld by every other principle in the universe; it *contains* every principle, it is *contained by* every principle.

It is possible to start from any point (the particular) and end up with the whole (the universal). This is a trick which has been implicitly sought by every philosopher in history, realized by none. It requires a knowledge of everything; for, to pontificate on any point, you have to adduce the whole; and to pontificate on the whole, you have to adduce the point. Any point will do, the particular point representing all points.

All points represent the whole, the whole represents all points. Taking any particular, physical object (or point), what relationship has it to the inner world of mind (the universal)? In the first place, it obviously represents the physical, therefore outside, world; hence we have outer facing inner. What does one do as a consequence? Does one shut up shop and say, "they can't be reconciled?" It is precisely because Western philosophy, and even Eastern philosophy, has resolutely ignored the relation of inner to outer, that the most fundamental problems of the universe have never been resolved; they have never been addressed.

Inner and outer are a couple of bed mates, the one—inner—reflecting the other—outer—and vice-versa. Any external object, or point, is juxtaposed with the internal world, or mind—no-one would dispute that, except that the external world is not generally regarded as consisting of points. *But I have illustrated elsewhere that the internal world is contiguous, while the external world does consist of fractured points—or individual points.* The 'universal', or inner world of mind, consists of unity—a fact endorsed, despite itself, by science, which points out the background unity of the universe while at the same time reserving this for the physical universe alone—which is of course nonsense. Because of its blinkered ability to see, science contradicts itself manfully, along with our friends, the Buddhist monks.

Firstly, the Buddhists maintain that there are no individual objects—given that, according to them, there is no such thing as individuality. They maintain, at the same time, that there is no difference between the inside and outside worlds—that there exists nothing but the inside world. Buddhists make this point because, firstly, they believe in the overwhelming unity of the universe, that being *inner*, and because, secondly, *their belief cannot admit the existence of individual phenomena, or objects*—an egotistical, and collective, religious quirk.

The contradiction in all this is rife and obvious. Both science and Buddhism cannot—or dare not—see the glaring truth that we are faced, in each instance, with a paradox: that science cannot see *the identification* of mind and the outer world, and Buddhism cannot see *the difference*.

We have objects, or the outside world, on the one hand, and mind, or the inside world, on the other; no-one in his right mind would dispute this alignment. But neither science nor Buddhism is in its right mind. The contiguous unity of the internal, or universal, world is contrasted with the individual dis-unity of the external, or particular world. On the one hand, science cannot see the internal world because of its preoccupation with physical objects; on the other, Buddhism cannot see the external world because of its fascination with mind.

Beauty Is Truth And Truth Beauty

But we are here to be conscious as well as to experience pleasure, and so, in support of this, we emerge regularly into the daylight to gaze upon each other in wonder: at our own beauty. Pausing to take stock, we converse verbally whereas, a few moments before, our conversation had been conducted by bodily communication only; love-making consists of precisely that: the art of conversation. The thing that marks us off from animals is consciousness, particularly the ability to consciously contemplate beauty; and beauty is itself the inspiration to making love. I fuck you because you are beautiful—not because you happen to have a body. "Beauty is truth, and truth beauty"; these two things we find in sex— in pleasure. Pleasure was invented precisely for the purpose of the conscious and unconscious contemplation of beauty; in unconsciousness we know truth, in consciousness we see truth.

Unconscious knowledge and conscious knowledge together go so far as to make the Supra-Conscious—the final goal of sex. Within the sexual act lies the whole meaning and purpose of life—waiting to be explored through the antimony of spirit and pleasure (or flesh).

*   *   *

I think I have finally proved, by a digressive route, that the universe does consist of mind. Consistence alone would establish it, while forays into the byways of metaphysics set the seal on it.

Divine Love II

<u>*The Ultimate Point Of The Christian Religion, upon which it becomes the Antonian religion: the self-revelation of God—of his love, to his world.*</u>

In God's love, his sexuality is the most obvious expression. In presenting his sexuality—not my sexuality—to the world, I am providing the evidence of that love.

I bring—*as the representative of God*—explicit sex, explicit pleasure, to man and woman for the first time. The opposites have never before been separated.

In demonstrating, through his love, explicit sexuality, God risks alienating the whole of humanity, and Christ's psychological crucifixion will thereby be re-enforced. The messenger, as ever, will be shot.

Appearances are deceptive; an inalienable and profound

truth—so profound that God finds it necessary to send his son into the world to convey it, specifically through sexual intercourse. A gob smacking image—and chosen for precisely that reason.

God conveys his truth by shock, and what could be more shocking than the crucifixion of his own son, whether physically or psychologically?—quintessentially through the most intimate act possible. *The most physical act possible conveys the greatest truth possible: the total illusion of the physical world, and physical existence itself. What could be more appropriate than the presentation of this ultimate symbol of physicality? It sums up, doesn't it, the most obscene example of physicality?—sheer, physical lust—which Christ has come specifically to destroy—not to promote.*

In exhibiting this symbol, therefore, Christ is proclaiming his horror at the whole idea of physical sexuality—the very reverse of what it appears to be.

Throughout his life, Christ has been in the habit of demonstrating the truth by appearing to demonstrate the exact opposite. *This is designed to make people think.* And because psychiatrists, in particular, *don't think*, Christ started off his lifelong career of crucifixion by inadvertently declaring to them that he 'heard voices'— *the exact opposite of the truth.* Christ had convinced himself that no-one could possibly be so unutterably stupid as to believe something so obviously untrue, which, if those psychiatrists had been capable of thinking, they wouldn't have done.

Christ, or Anthony Hill, has never in his life exhibited any symptoms of schizophrenia, whether by behaviour or otherwise, as those psychiatrists should have known by observation alone. So, being faced with such an obvious declaration of untruth, what does our expert do *but abandon all pretensions to thought.* Even before I had opened my mouth, he had already assumed I was ill—quite without reason or evidence, *but from the mere fact that I was in his clinic.* And right from the start, he was not prepared to accept any evidence that I wasn't. Psychiatrists do that—because any suggestion of professional incompetence, however slight, gets right at their ego.

The application of thinking, dismissed from his mind by his own ego, would have alerted him to the fact that here was a man so obviously intelligent, and devoid of any sign of mental illness—as he had observed on his ward—that there was no possibility of his being schizophrenic. But then, he *doesn't* think—he just observes myopically, and on the basis of what he sees, or hears, makes an unconsidered decision from *surface appearance alone.*

As a result, Anthony Hill was precipitated into his lifelong crucifixion at the hands of psychiatry. *And surface appearance has kept him there, in the mind of humankind, right up to the present day*, when his crucifixion is about to be relieved by that terrible image—the image of God himself having intercourse—so untrue that it proves the opposite.

The world is so absolutely ruled by superficiality, that no truth survives. The surface of physical existence disguises reality from man to the extent that he is unaware of the basic facts of life. *He himself disguises himself from himself; consciousness is hidden by unconsciousness.*

The one thing above all that I am seeking for, in sex, or love, is 'ultimate reality'—or 'ultimate truth'; that is, *self-knowledge.* "Know thyself", is the dictum—specifically through the study of spirit and pleasure, or the Mother-Whore antinomy. This antinomy, above all other principles in the Cosmos, was set up expressly for that purpose. Love itself was created for two equal reasons: the *expression* of self, and the *knowledge* of self; and, from that, the knowledge of Cosmic reality: the very nature of God himself.

And God has come before man to expose himself as love—through sex, but not as sex; for sex is the ultimate illusion, having been reduced by man to a loveless, momentary physical orgasm—so dirty as to necessitate the utmost personal demonstration of Love's truth—and, with it, the absolute innocence of your Saviour, who degraded himself for a lifetime, out of his boundless love, in order to save you.

So, a lifetime for one degrading, yet glorious, moment. The glory for which it was given saves the degradation *by* which it was given. The illusion of physical existence is revealed; do not, therefore, 'judge by appearances'. The horror of Christ's experience had to be: to demonstrate the truth of beauty, and the beauty of truth.

*   *   *

What people will balk at is the physical, superficial appearance. The masses will never accept the proof of reality; all they are concerned about is the apparent evidence to their senses, being convinced by *their ego* that they are absolutely right, and that Christ himself is wrong. And they will believe that in the face of all proof, *precisely because they are determined to hate him*. The salacious nature of the common man leads him to believe that everybody, including the Son of God, is of that ilk.

"I know what I see", says Joe. His ego will never allow him to acknowledge that anyone could be so superior as to transcend all physical appearances. "Facts are facts", of course, and unless the world realizes that, actually, facts are not facts, and never, in the real world, *could* be facts,

Christ is likely to be condemned for ever—a fact to which he is used—even from his own sweetheart.

Finale

In the end, all opposites return to each other—the same, but different—irrevocably changed but still bearing their essential character. *So changed are they that, eventually, they turn into each other; they become each other.* Good becomes evil, evil becomes good; the mother becomes the whore, the whore becomes the mother. The innocent whore becomes the illicit whore, and vice-versa. *No-one can tell the difference, because the dirty bitch is, and always has been, the essence of innocence.*

Good and evil finally become one, in Absolute Good, or Absolute Love. God returns to himself, as the Absolute Good itself, having journeyed to earth and become evil, for the sake of his people.

Good triumphs after all.

Appendix

It may or may not have been perceived that the stress from 'love' to 'spirit' in regard to consciousness has been altered during the progress of the book; having started with the declaration that love, in explicit sex, was designed to be unconscious, the book ends with the plea that love should after all be conscious and that it is spirit—or the 'good' spirit—which should remain in the unconscious mode. For love is the Third Element and as such contains both the good *and bad* spirits, each of which remains unconscious in favour of the other according to whichever is emphasized during either platonic sex or explicit sex. Love is *always* conscious, but the good spirit, in explicit sex, should be unconsciously perceived, while the bad spirit, or the spirit of pleasure, should remain unemphasized during platonic sex.

Forthcoming Titles

1. *The Revolutionising of Medical Procedure ,Physical and Mental: A Theoretical Outline.*

2. *Parsifal's Journal, Issue II.*
   Neo-Christian Metaphysics in the Second Millennium.

3. *Professor Anthony's Casebook; A Damsel in Distress.*
   Forming an investigation into the pitfalls of life. An erotic novel and philosophical exegesis combined.

4. *The Revival of the Self, or The Transformation of Evil.*
   A Psychological Exposition.

5. An Oblique Approach to Wagnerian Psychology: *An Investigation into its Implications.*

6. *Woman: Mother and Whore*
   Man: Father and Rake
   A sequel to *The Sanctity and Profanity of Sexuality.*

7. *Art Through Knowledge, Knowledge Through Art.*
   A very practical artistic and philosophical synthesis
   with step by step instructions.

8. *Professor Anthony's Casebook;*
   Pursuing the Mother, Pursuing the Father.
   A young couple's traumatic search for their sexual
   identities: a novel combined with philosophy.

9. *The Universal Schism and the Perversion of*
   Schizophrenia.
   A psychological exposition.

10. *Through Christian Eyes: Towards an Integration of*
    World Religions.
    A psychological exposition.

11. *Parsifal's Journal, Issue III.*
    Neo-Christian Metaphysics in the Second
    Millennium.

12. *Tony Hill's Autobiography: The Man in the Iron Mask.*
    An Account of Psychiatry versus Truth.

13. *The Cosmos and Planet Earth: A Brief Survey.*

14. *Erotic Excerpts.*

15. *Parsifal's Journal, Issue IV.*
    Neo-Christian Metaphysics in the Second
    Millennium.